GREAT CAREERS IN THE SPORTS INDUSTRY™

DREAM JOBS IN COACHING

COLLEEN RYCKERT COOK

ROSEN PUBLISHING®
New York

Published in 2013 by The Rosen Publishing Group, Inc.
29 East 21st Street, New York, NY 10010

Copyright © 2013 by The Rosen Publishing Group, Inc.

First Edition

All rights reserved. No part of this book may be reproduced in any form without permission in writing from the publisher, except by a reviewer.

Library of Congress Cataloging-in-Publication Data

Cook, Colleen Ryckert.
Dream jobs in coaching/Colleen Ryckert Cook.
  p. cm.—(Great careers in the sports industry)
Includes bibliographical references and index.
ISBN 978-1-4488-6903-9 (library binding)
1. Coaching (Athletics)—Vocational guidance. I. Title.
GV711.C74 2012
796.07'7—dc23
                                                    2011048597

Manufactured in the United States of America

CPSIA Compliance Information: Batch #S12YA: For further information, contact Rosen Publishing, New York, New York, at 1-800-237-9932.

CONTENTS

Introduction	4
CHAPTER 1 **Coaching's Role in the Community**	8
CHAPTER 2 **Getting the Jump in High School**	19
CHAPTER 3 **Lay the Groundwork at College**	29
CHAPTER 4 **Sports Instructors and Community Coaches**	39
CHAPTER 5 **Coaching Middle Grade and High School**	50
CHAPTER 6 **Coaching at the Collegiate Level**	60
CHAPTER 7 **Coaching a Professional Team**	72
CHAPTER 8 **Coaching Individual Sports**	84
College and University Programs in Coaching and Physical Fitness	94
A Career in Coaching at a Glance	96
Bureau of Labor Statistics Information	99
Glossary	105
For More Information	108
For Further Reading	113
Bibliography	116
Index	120

INTRODUCTION

Kansas University's men's basketball coach Bill Self started his coaching career at KU as an assistant under Larry Brown in 1985. He returned as head coach in 2003 and led the Jayhawks to multiple titles.

INTRODUCTION

Nestled in the University of Kansas's Allen Fieldhouse, just a short walk to the famed James Naismith Court, is the office of the men's varsity basketball coach, Bill Self. Self is one of the more successful college coaches in the game today. In the first eight years of his taking over the Kansas program in 2003, Self amassed seven Big 12 Conference regular season championship titles, five Big 12 tournament championship titles, and the 2008 NCAA National Championship.

Self's office is packed with mementos of the Kansas Jayhawks' many accomplishments. There's the hardwood, glass-topped box packed with championships rings. There's a photograph of Self's family and the 2008 national championship team meeting President George W. Bush. Five etched crystal tournament championship trophies weigh down his built-in glass shelves, as do two marble and Waterford crystal awards from the National Association of Basketball Coaches, one for the 2008 Jayhawks and one for Danny Manning and the Miracles' win in 1988. Then there are the two sleek gold-plated John Wooden Awards for KU's 1988 and 2008 championship wins.

But if you ask Self to point out his favorite memento, he won't choose any of those trophies. He won't even point to a handwritten note from the Boss himself, Bruce Springsteen, congratulating the team for their 2008 win. No, Self will point to a photograph of four players—two in Kansas jerseys in the center, flanked by two North Carolina Tar Heels, all four diving for a loose ball.

At first glance it looks like a great action shot caught at the perfect tournament moment, until Self points out what makes it so special to him.

Four bodies. Six hands. One ball.

The North Carolina players each have one hand on the ball and their other hand bracing themselves for a hard slam against the wood floor. The two Kansas players—Darnell Jackson and Darrell Arthur—have both hands wrapped around the ball. No hands free to break their fall.

That photo embodies the qualities Self wants in his teams. That's what he teaches during hours and hours of practice. That's what he's looking for as he sifts through reports on thousands of potential high school and junior college basketball players. He will reach out to several hundred of them, ask for highlight videos, and whittle his list further until he has a few dozen players in mind. They must possess the skills he needs, whether to fill a void, grow into a leadership role, or create a deeper bench. He'll invite them to basketball camp. He'll woo them with tours of the campus and fieldhouse. He'll show them what they can accomplish if they become part of his team.

If he does his job right, his top choices will sign letters of intent to play at Allen Fieldhouse.

As a Division 1 coach at a university with such a storied and esteemed basketball past, Self is expected to bring in top talent, to come out on top of the Big 12 conference and tournaments, to make a strong showing in the NCAA tournament.

But a coach's purpose goes beyond winning games. Coaches teach skills and rules, of course, and motivate their players to perform at their very best. But coaches also provide psychological and emotional support. They ensure an athlete's skills are built through proper physical conditioning. They understand when and how to push harder. Those coaching qualities matter at the upper echelons of professional sports all the way down to peewee camps.

Chapter 1
COACHING'S ROLE IN THE COMMUNITY

The twentieth century brought a tidal wave of technological advances that seemed to swell as the century moved closer to a new millennium. People moved off the farms and into towns and cities. They found jobs with workdays that went from nine to five, five days a week. This gave them more leisure time than they'd ever enjoyed before.

This new free time coincided with a resurgence of the Olympics in the early 1900s. The two factors brought an increased interest in physical fitness and personal best performances as well. Organized sports grew in popularity in the first half of the twentieth century. High school and college game days drew fans by the hundreds and thousands, and later by the tens of thousands.

By the 1980s, public gymnasiums—the sweaty, smelly dominion of boxers and weight lifters—had turned into glossy, carpeted classrooms filled with pop music and

COACHING'S ROLE IN THE COMMUNITY

At the 1936 Olympic Games in Berlin, Germany, African American athletes like gold medal–winning track star Cornelius Johnson fought hatred with physical heroics. The fire was fanned by the motivation and encouragement of the Olympic team coaches.

leotard-clad exercisers of both sexes. Youth sports camps flourished through local parks and recreation departments. Community athletic fields sprung up across the nation.

Today, children and adults everywhere are swinging hockey sticks and tennis rackets, dribbling basketballs and lobbing volleyballs, swimming, diving, jogging, riding, gliding over ice and down slopes, kicking balls, catching pop flies, and throwing long. It's a great habit to get into as a youngster and a positive lifestyle choice well into adulthood. These influences are then passed on to future generations.

And this means the demand for good coaches keeps growing.

IT'S JUST A GAME

Some people might not fully recognize what a coach does. Sports and other athletic activities are supposed to be just for fun, they might say. Don't take it so seriously. It's not life or death.

True, and yet athletics are essential to community health.

While many people fill their increased leisure hours with sports or other physical activity, many others opt to settle in on the couch or recliner and watch from the sidelines. Study after study shows how public health issues such as increased diabetes, high blood pressure, and heart disease are related to physical inactivity. These chronic conditions cost millions of dollars each year, with many of the expenses footed by the public.

These studies also show that adults who are active have lower incidences of health problems. How active people are as adults often has much to do with how active they were as children. A 2010 study reported in the *International Journal of Behavioral Nutrition and Physical Activity* studied how adults engaged in physical activity during their leisure time. Researchers asked participants whether they played competitive sports in

COACHING'S ROLE IN THE COMMUNITY

their youth. Did they continue exercising during their adolescence? What were their opinions about physical education programs?

They found that whether people participated in sports and academic clubs as children had a direct effect on how those adults spent their leisure time. People who played sports as children and supported physical education efforts as adults tended to be more physically active as adults.

Children join contact sports at younger ages, like these seven- and eight-year-old tackle football players. Growing bodies and minds need exceptional coaches. They need teachers who understand what young players need to develop skills.

11

The researchers note more study is needed to confirm their initial findings, but it makes sense. An emphasis on physical activity and good health early in life leads to active, healthy lives with each passing year.

It seems like a huge no-brainer—athletic children grow up to be athletic adults. But this isn't always the case. The researchers also found that socioeconomic factors contributed to unhealthy adult behaviors, including physical inactivity. In other words, uneducated people and those living in poverty tended to be less physically active in general than people who are better educated and live above the poverty level.

Some will say this means communities need affordable sports opportunities for children of all economic and educational backgrounds. Ideally these opportunities will start in elementary school and continue through high school. This can be difficult to put into practice, as many public school systems across the nation face budget restraints. Parks and recreation sports leagues or those offered through groups like the YMCA that seek out volunteer coaches can help. Volunteers keep expenses low and fees affordable.

We know physical activity leads to better health. It decreases the risk of death from cardiovascular disease, reduces blood pressure, and controls body weight and blood sugar levels. Certain physical activities improve bone mass and health, maintain muscle strength, and

COACHING'S ROLE IN THE COMMUNITY

COACHES' SPOTLIGHT: JOHN GAGLIARDI, FOOTBALL, ST. JOHN'S UNIVERSITY

478–129–11. Those three simple numbers are St. John's University football coach John Gagliardi's record going into the 2011 season—his sixty-third as head coach. Since 1953, he's led the Division III Johnnies to victory, including four national championships and twenty-six conference titles. His approach to football—and to building a winning program—contradicts what most coaches preach:

- No tackling in practice.
- No blocking sleds or dummies.
- No compulsory weight lifting program.
- No whistles.
- No "Coach"—players call him John.
- No long practices—ninety minutes or less.
- No athletic scholarships.

In his first year at St. John's, Gagliardi took a team most people believed couldn't win to the Minnesota Intercollegiate Athletic Conference (MIAC) title. But that's not all. He led the St. John's track team to a championship that same school year. In five years as hockey coach, he racked up a 42–25–1 record, still the best career winning percentage of any hockey coach in school history. He even has a trophy named after him: the Gagliardi Trophy goes to the nation's outstanding Division III player.

His career started in 1943 when he was a sixteen-year-old team captain at Holy Trinity High School in

Trinidad, Colorado. He took over coaching when the team's actual coach was drafted into World War II and quickly got rid of the drills he disliked most as a player. No calisthenics. No wind sprints. He let players drink water during practice.

He didn't know what he was doing, he once said. He just did what he thought was right. He wanted an atmosphere where players could concentrate on what he calls the critical point and execute flawless plays.

His "no" formula still works. In 2006, Gagliardi became the only active coach inducted into the College Football Hall of Fame. He still shows up each day before 8:00 AM to watch films. He is still revered by players and opponents alike. His all-time winning record likely won't be broken anytime soon.

build coordination. Exercise also improves cognitive functioning. It enhances the immune system and builds self-esteem.

In other words, it's a huge factor in physical and mental health. Better overall health means lower medical costs, which will help ease the strain on tax-supported health systems. There are also claims that residents in good physical health make for stronger communities. People participate in community building. They give more, reach out to others, and foster strong, connected neighborhoods.

COACHING'S ROLE IN THE COMMUNITY

PROFESSIONAL COACHING ORGANIZATIONS AND ASSOCIATIONS

Professional organizations and associations can help people build their careers, provide continuing education, and offer insight into a chosen business. Coaches also get support through various organizations.

There are coach associations by state and by sport, and they are even divided up by volunteer coaches, high school coaches, college coaches, and so on. A simple online search will turn up dozens or more.

The North American Society for Sports Management is an organization for coaches working in any sport, whether for business or leisure. It offers insight into sports management, including marketing, fundraising, leadership development, sports and the law, employment opportunities, and more. It offers an official research journal, the *Journal of Sports Management*. Articles cover such topics as organizational strategies, finance and accounting, public relations and media communication, and facility and event management.

THE REAL ROLE OF A COACH

All coaches want to win, but good coaches know a team can't win without knowing the strategies and movements of a game. Coaches, therefore, are teachers first and foremost. They teach players how to move their bodies to

Dream Jobs in Coaching

Team sports need coaches who understand interpersonal dynamics, can recognize individual strengths and apply them to a group goal, and motivate athletes to put aside their egos for the good of the team.

accomplish a specific task. They teach them how to use equipment properly and how to build specific muscle groups for specific tasks.

They also teach players how to keep their heads in the game. Pushing the body physically wears a person down mentally and emotionally. A coach is there to direct players down the right path. The best coaches provide direction, motivation, and support. They teach skills and good sportsmanship. They encourage players to give their physical and mental best each time they hit the court, floor, field, ice, water, or hill—whatever the sport may be.

Good coaches must understand the psychology behind coaching. It isn't about yelling on the sidelines or making athletes run laps if practice goes badly. Coaching goes beyond calling plays or managing workout routines. It is more than watching tapes of opponents and finding weaknesses to manipulate.

For individual sports, coaches concentrate on skills and the mental toughness needed by athletes who are on the line by themselves, solely bearing the weight of an entire match or performance. Good coaches learn to find a player's internal motivation to succeed. They recognize signs when a player is experiencing mental burnout. They formulate a training plan to maximize the years their athlete can stay in the game, and they adjust to accommodate changes over time.

For team sports, coaches observe players closely to figure out their particular strengths and shortcomings. They must know the kind of physical and mental ability needed for each position on the team. They must take a group of individuals and foster a sense of unity and mutual goals. They set goals for their teams to accomplish in the season. They must look at long-term goals as well. High school and college coaches need to know where their team will be in four years when the newest players will be graduates. Professional coaches need to be aware of contracts and individual career desires of their players. In some cases, they must factor in salary caps and budget restrictions when finding new team members.

Coaches need the insight of a psychologist, the stubbornness of a drill sergeant, and the physical stamina of the very athletes they are guiding. They need insight into the dynamics of opponents. Plus, they need a genuine love and excitement for the sport.

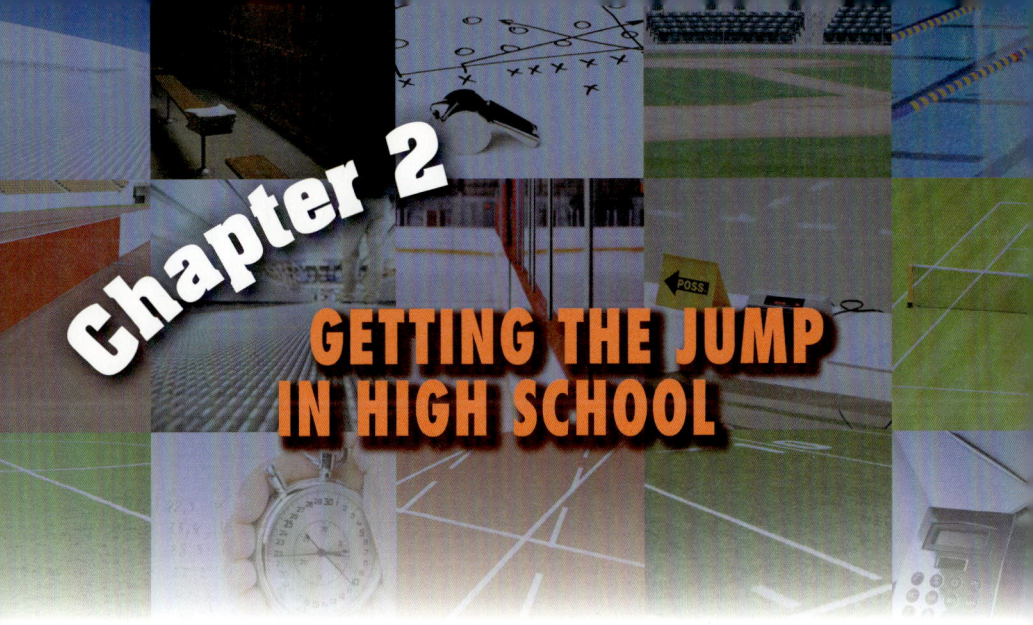

Chapter 2
GETTING THE JUMP IN HIGH SCHOOL

High school is a great time to start laying the foundation for your future as a coach. Many high school students who think they might want to coach for a career likely play several sports. This is a great way to understand the dynamics of a given sport's rules and strategies. Some players play only one sport. This is also a valuable experience, as the athlete learns so much more about the sport, such as the way the body performs in that sport and the nutrition and conditioning needed to succeed. A downside to such specialization: a future coach might be exposed to only a few coaching styles. This doesn't give as broad a range of experience with different coaching styles that multisport players get.

WHAT MAKES A GREAT LEADER?

It might seem like only the very best athletes can move into a coaching position, but the truth is that the best coaches weren't necessarily athletic standouts.

Dream Jobs in Coaching

COACHES' SPOTLIGHT: NANABAH ALLISON-BREWER, VOLLEYBALL, SOUTH DAKOTA STATE UNIVERSITY

Nanabah Allison-Brewer had big dreams as a young Navajo girl in Farmington, New Mexico. She played volleyball with passion and determination. Her talents took her to New Mexico State, where she earned a degree in statistics and played on the volleyball team for four years. At Arizona State University she earned a master's degree in education and cut her coaching teeth as a volunteer assistant coach for the men's basketball team. Next Allison-Brewer went on to the Ivy League halls of Dartmouth, where she served as the women's assistant volleyball coach and recruiting coordinator before the University of South Dakota nabbed her in 2006. Today, she is one of just a few Native Americans who coach or play at the Division 1 level.

Some of her accomplishments:

- Four varsity letters as a player with the University of New Mexico from 1995 to 1999, where she compiled 1,005 digs and 195 service aces in 417 games.

- Played on the 1997 Lobo women's basketball team that won the Western Athletic Conference (WAC) postseason title and advanced to the NCAA Tournament.

- The 1998 WAC Defensive Specialist of the Year

- Represented the U.S. Olympic Committee at the International Olympic Academy held in Olympia, Greece, in 1998.

GETTING THE JUMP IN HIGH SCHOOL

- The 1999 Native American Sports Council's Woman Sport Warrior of the Year.
- Ranked eighth at New Mexico in career digs and in career service aces when she graduated in 2000.
- Arizona Grand Canyon District 4A Coach of the Year, 2000
- New Mexico District 1-4A Coach of the Year, 2001
- Played on a Native American volleyball team that won the gold medal at the North American Indigenous Games in Denver, Colorado, in 2006.

The accolades are nice, but the accomplishment she is most proud of is the Native American Volleyball Academy she helped found in 2007. Allison-Brewer worked with former Haskell Indian Nations University recruiter Judith Ginn to bring together Native American girls playing high school and junior high volleyball for a three-day intensive camp. The purpose was more than to teach them skills. It was more than to help Ginn recruit players. It was Allison-Brewer's way to show these girls what they can accomplish with determination and drive and to give them the knowledge to achieve it. She wanted to teach them the standards needed to play at the collegiate level and how the recruiting process works. The coaches of the camp are all now Native American women. They inspire their players to dream big and fly higher.

Dream Jobs in Coaching

Take famed football coach Vince Lombardi. He might never have been the legend he is today had things gone according to his original life plan. Lombardi played baseball and basketball as a fifteen-year-old studying for the priesthood at the Cathedral College of the Immaculate Conception. He'd say he wasn't very good at those sports. He had bad eyesight. He was also small, around 5 feet, 8 inches (1.8 m) tall. But he was stocky, with fire in his blood. And he loved football. He played off-campus on the sly because it was against Cathedral College's rules.

After two years it became clear the priesthood wasn't for him. Seventeen-year-old Lombardi transferred to St.

How do you keep a team of individual standouts cohesive when they compete against other teams and their own teammates? Swimming, gymnastics, and other similar sports need coaches who can successfully lead a team and coach individual personal bests.

Francis Prep School and played football there. His determination and passion on the field earned him respect from coaches and fellow players.

After graduation, Lombardi attended Fordham University and become one of Fordham's famed "Seven Blocks of Granite" on the football team. He graduated magna cum laude in 1937 and attended law school for a time. But he couldn't stay away from the sport he loved so much, and before long he left his law aspirations behind to take on a teaching and assistant football coaching position at St. Cecilia High School in Englewood, New Jersey.

Lombardi also coached at his alma mater, Fordham University, for two years before moving on to work as an assistant coach under Red Blaik at West Point in 1949. In the next years Lombardi developed a coaching style that became synonymous with his name: simplicity and execution. He was a tireless workaholic. In time he became an assistant coach in the National Football League (NFL) for the New York Giants. The Giants enjoyed five winning seasons and won the league championship in 1956.

Lombardi became the golden boy of coaching, and in January 1959 he accepted the head coaching position with the Green Bay Packers. The rest, as they say, is history.

The trophy handed to the Super Bowl's winning team is called the Lombardi Trophy for a reason. Lombardi was an unstoppable force. His training camps were arduous. He demanded total commitment and the hardest effort

Dream Jobs in Coaching

The Green Bay Packers hoist head coach Vince Lombardi after winning the 1966 NFL Championship Game. The Lombardi Trophy, presented to the Super Bowl winner, is named in his honor.

from his players. Under his guidance, the Green Bay Packers won five NFL Championships, including victories in Super Bowl I and II. After a two-year break from coaching, Lombardi returned to lead the Washington Redskins in 1969, promptly taking them to their first winning season in more than a decade. He died much too young the following year of colon cancer. He was fifty-seven years old.

According to the Lombardi Web site, he once said, "It is essential to understand that battles are primarily won in the hearts of men. Men respond to leadership in a most remarkable way, and once you have won his heart he will follow you anywhere."

COACHES' SPOTLIGHT: RORY WHIPPLE, LACROSSE, UNIVERSITY OF TAMPA

Though lacrosse is played throughout North America and Canada, it is off the radar for many sports fans. If Rory Whipple has his way, that will change.

The University of Tampa added lacrosse to its athletic offerings in spring 2012. And when it comes to winning, UT doesn't mess around. Its teams have won twelve NCAA Division II National Championships and a whopping seventy-two first-place conference finishes.

Whipple's certainly no slouch. He is the all-time winningest lacrosse coach in the NCAA. UT is the fourth school to ask him to kick-start their lacrosse program. Unlike football, basketball, and other high-profile sports, lacrosse programs often come with no scholarship funding. Still, he's managed to lead no-scholarship players to defeat better-established teams in championship games. A lot of his success comes from his longevity and wins in the sport. As head coach of the Iroquois National team in 1994, he led his team to fifth place at the World Lacrosse Championship in England.

Whipple has the experience to lure talent and the connections to build a strong program. Building a team from the ground up requires a special focus on recruiting. He must sort through the freshmen who've already been accepted. He must seek out other potential players at high schools and junior colleges. And that is part of the thrill he gets, why he is willing to leave a growing, even successful program at one school to start fresh at another. He can build the team he wants, from coaches to players. He can set standards and long-term goals. And he can introduce his beloved sport to new lacrosse fans.

Not everyone can hack it as a coach. The best coaches are natural motivators. They understand team dynamics and the mental aspects of playing competitively. They know the sport inside and out and recognize what skills are needed when and where. Coaching requires its own special skills and talents.

PREP WORK

So what can teens do now to prepare for a coaching career? First, play. Play a lot. Play for fun and play competitively under good coaches. Take up a sport you've never played before. Learn everything you can about all the positions and the best strategies for those positions to succeed. Watch how other athletes approach their game. What motivates them? What causes them to lose their cool?

Perhaps the best thing you can do is to observe the coaches around you. What do they do that works well? What aspects of their coaching style don't work so well or contradict how you would want to try it? You can draw from their best qualities and get a feel for how much you need to learn.

Then volunteer. Give your time and knowledge to help teams playing through local community centers, country clubs, parks and recreation departments, or church or other youth group programs. Teens can serve as teaching assistants, managers, even assistant coaches.

GETTING THE JUMP IN HIGH SCHOOL

Ball boys at the 2011 U.S. Open tennis tournament in New York, N.Y., watch the game closely. They are able to watch the very best athletes succeed and fail, and they see how many coaches interact with their players.

Teens can also start taking high school classes that apply to coaching: anatomy, physical education, communication studies, weight lifting, psychology, and sociology if the school offers them. Another course you might not have thought about taking is one that teaches about foods and nutrition; what kind of diet does a high-performance athlete need to succeed? Activities that emphasize leadership development, such as debate team or student council, can help as well.

If your school district doesn't offer these types of classes at the high school level, consider taking a summer course at a local community college. Summer camps can be another great learning experience. Camp counselors work with a variety of personalities. They must teach skills to children with varying levels of internal motivation and skills. They must make teaching fun to foster a love of the activity. They must break down complex rules to help children understand the concepts. They must also break down the physical movements necessary to kick a ball, or catch one, or swing a club or racket so that a beginner can easily follow along.

Teens can get a broad idea of what goes on in the sporting industry by holding other sports-related part-time jobs, too. Working behind the concession stand might not seem like a way to hone your coaching skills, but coaches will see the dedication and initiative. You will make an impression that can lead to volunteer assistant positions.

Many teens work part-time in groundskeeping or as equipment managers. Tennis enthusiasts help out at professional opens and matches by working as ball boys and girls and towel boys and girls. You can help man the tables at sign-up and registration. You can volunteer as a scorekeeper, timekeeper, umpire, or lifeguard.

These noncoaching jobs will expose you to a broader picture of what the sports industry means to players and spectators. You will see the very best and the very worst sides of competitive sports and the families and fans who watch them. That experience will help give you the mental toughness, the fortitude, and the resolution to become the kind of coach you want to be.

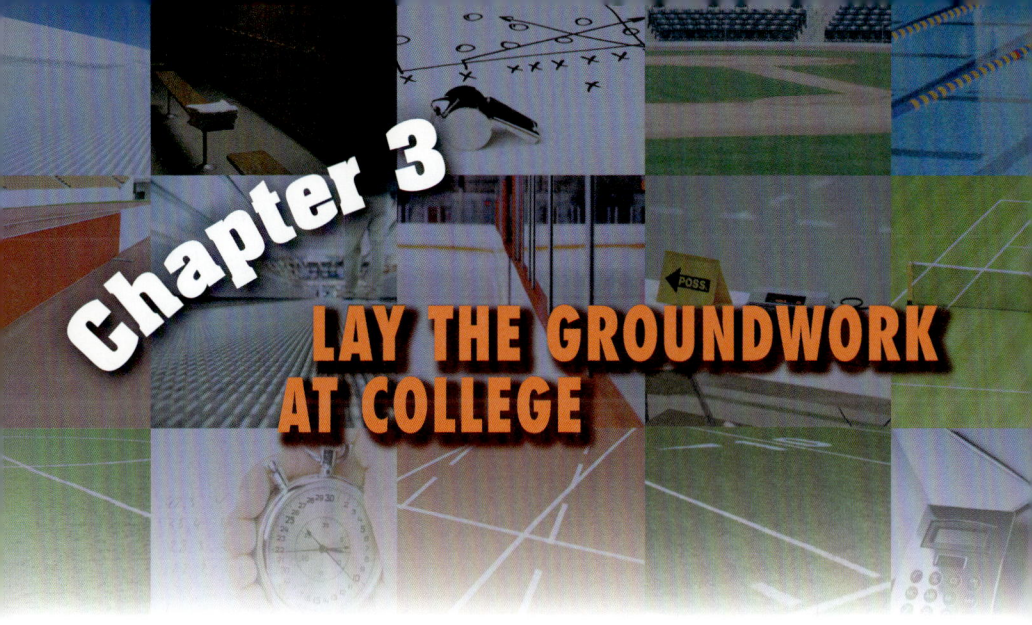

Chapter 3
LAY THE GROUNDWORK AT COLLEGE

Some people have the remarkable gift of knowing exactly what they want to do with their lives. Their path is lit up with runway lights, pointing out which college courses to take and what opportunities to nab. Others have a general idea—"I'd like to do this as a career"—but aren't always exactly sure how to go about getting there.

For students who believe they are destined to be great coaches, there are other issues they must think about before sending their résumé off to the Yankees main office. If you want to coach, you need to consider the best path to get there.

Most coaches have a college degree and even a master's degree. They realize the high-end coaching jobs at Division I schools and professional teams are fleeting at best. While it's true that top universities and professional teams have extensive coaching staffs, the number of coaches overall who make a comfortable living by just coaching is miniscule.

College coaches at smaller schools—Division II, Division III and so on—often have multiple roles. Sometimes they teach. Sometimes they serve as athletic directors or in marketing services. Sometimes they coach multiple sports. To succeed, a future coach must be prepared.

BODYWORKS

The obvious answer for students who hope to coach is to seek a bachelor's degree in physical education. It certainly makes sense. Coaching is about physical excellence. Lots of coaches are also teachers, particularly at the community and high school level. Teacher certification isn't a job guarantee after graduation, but it opens more opportunities.

For a physical education major, students focus on anatomy to study the human body and skeleton. They learn how the cardiovascular system works and the effects of exercise and calories. Exercise physiology covers how the body functions and reacts to movement and muscle development, including changes in metabolism. Courses on motor development and motor learning and the sociology of team sports prepare a future teacher to be a coach as well as educator. Ethics courses are also crucial for future role models.

A degree in physical education isn't necessary, but it is helpful. Many high school coaches teach physical education, as each role flows well into the other.

LAY THE GROUNDWORK AT COLLEGE

Coaching community programs can be great for college students. You get hands-on experience in a low-stress setting and learn firsthand how to work and motivate people with a variety of skills.

BLACK COACHES AND ADMINISTRATORS

Jesse Owens takes off at the start of the 200-meter race at the 1936 Olympic Games in Berlin. That summer Owens won four gold medals.

Desegregation in early and mid-twentieth-century America took time. Sports fields and courts were some of the first places where minorities could succeed alongside whites in this changing culture.

Jesse Owens blazed past the competition at the 1936 Berlin Olympics. He won four gold medals, broke eleven Olympic records, and soared above the notion of white superiority. Jackie Robinson broke color barriers on the baseball diamond in 1946 when he became the first African American to play with whites. Two years earlier, African American coach John McLendon and his North Carolina Colored College's basketball team played "the secret game" with white coaches and players of Duke's Navy Medical School. Worried about Ku Klux Klan backlash, the schools kept spectators away. The teams, however, were happy to share a court.

In 1961, seven years after the *Brown v. Board of Education* Supreme Court decision and five years after the Montgomery bus boycott, Syracuse University's Ernie Davis became the first African American college football

LAY THE GROUNDWORK AT COLLEGE

player to win the Heisman Trophy. That same year, Wilt Chamberlain's 100-point game with the Philadelphia Warriors flushed down the sewer any lingering belief that blacks couldn't keep up in a white man's game.

Many minority athletes shined in the later decades of the century, but the number of star coaches took longer to rise. The 1970s and 1980s saw more minorities as collegiate and professional coaches. Still, the percentages were small. In 1987, African American assistant coaches in professional basketball and football asked themselves what they could do to help other minority coaches succeed.

They formed the Black Coaches Association in 1987. Its goal: to help coaches of color find employment opportunities. As more minority coaches moved into bigger leadership roles, the group found it needed to expand its focus. In 2007 it unveiled its new name, Black Coaches and Administrators. This nonprofit association of ethnic minority coaches offers professional development and scholarships for minority students seeking a career in sports.

JUST MANAGE

Another sports-related field is sports management. Students who earn degrees in sports management learn about sports marketing, sport finance, and sport administration. Internship opportunities can put you on the

Dream Jobs in Coaching

Sports journalist Rick Reilly coordinated a group of sports management students for a service-based initiative program. Their task: Send $10 mosquito nets to malaria-riddled communities in Africa.

sidelines as well. They will learn about budget preparation and other business management tasks as well as public relations and mass media. Coursework covers general education classes and sports management classes.

Sports management is growing in popularity. Many programs are realizing sports management can and should go beyond just the sport itself. Sports and athletics are essential to community health, both physical and mental. By giving back to their communities, coaches, from the newest tee ball team to the grandest major league corporation, build a bond of trust, goodwill, and good sportsmanship.

That's where service learning programs can come into play.

Students apply the leadership and management skills they've learned to tackle specific community projects. For example, a group of sports management students worked out an action plan to help a community dealing with malaria.

LAY THE GROUNDWORK AT COLLEGE

A TIMELINE OF FIRSTS FOR AFRICAN AMERICAN COACHES

- First African Americans hired as professional sports team coaches in the big three sports:
  - Fritz Pollard, American Professional Football Association, Akron Pros, 1921
  - John McLendon, American Basketball League, Cleveland Pipers, 1961
  - Buck O'Neal, Major League Baseball, Chicago Cubs, 1962
- First college coach to win three consecutive NAIA titles: John McLendon, Tennessee State, 1957, 1958, 1959
- First African American coach to win the NBA championship: Bill Russell, Boston Celtics, 1968
- First African American NCAA Division I basketball coach: Will Robinson, Illinois State University; 1970
- First African American National Basketball Association general manager: Wayne Embry, Milwaukee Bucs, 1972
- First African American manager in Major League Baseball: Frank Robinson, Cleveland Indians, 1975
- First African American head football coach, NCAA Division I-A: Willie Jeffries, Wichita State University, 1979
- First African American inducted into the Basketball Hall of Fame as a coach: Clarence Gaines, Winston-Salem State University, 1982
- First African American coach to win the NCAA Men's Division I Basketball Championship: John Thompson, Georgetown, 1984

Dream Jobs in Coaching

- First African American NBA Coach of the Year: Don Chaney, Houston Rockets, 1991
- First African American NFL head coach in the Super Bowl (tie): Lovie Smith, Chicago Bears; Tony Dungy, Indianapolis Colts, 2007
- First African American NFL head coach to win the Super Bowl: Tony Dungy, Super Bowl XLI, 2007

They studied the problem, malaria, which is the leading cause of death for children under five in Africa. It kills millions each year.

A simple $10 mosquito net for a bed can save lives. This particular project was coordinated by *Sports Illustrated* columnist Rick Reilly in 2006. He urged people to donate nets. As he put it, "Not hoop nets, soccer nets, or lacrosse nets. Not New Jersey Nets or dot-nets or clarinets. Mosquito nets."

The program let the sports management students apply their skills to serve humanity on a grander scale. They had to figure out what kind of facility would best serve their fund-raising needs. They planned their budget and timeline. They figured out how many people they needed to accomplish their goals. They assigned specific tasks and found volunteers. They brainstormed entertainment, publicity, and sponsorships. They targeted their audience market and assessed marketing strategies.

They had concrete, measurable goals—donations, sponsorships, attendance, and so on. At the end of the service program they assessed their accomplishments. More important, they assessed how helping the greater good affected the way they felt about themselves and their future careers.

SO WHAT IS THE BEST COURSE TO TAKE?

Ultimately, the answer to that question depends upon you. For example, let's look again at the Kansas men's basketball coaching staff. Head coach Bill Self majored in business at Oklahoma State University before getting a master's degree in sports management. Assistant coach Joe Dooley earned a bachelor's degree in speech communication from George Washington University. Assistant coach Danny Manning earned a bachelor's degree in communications from KU. Barry Hinson, director of basketball operations, holds a bachelor's degree in secondary social sciences from OSU. As KU students, graduate assistant Brennan Bechard earned a bachelor's degree in sports management and video coordinator Jeff Forbes earned a bachelor's degree in English and a master's degree in education.

Pursue the study that excites you the most because this will be the gateway to your future. But there are other things you can do to network and gain more knowledge. If you aren't a collegiate player or don't have the contacts necessary to find opportunities, you will need to create your own. Volunteer or apply for positions at summer camps or a campus invitational. If you have the means, attend national clinics or apply for unpaid internships.

Seek out local high school or middle school programs and offer your volunteer services as well. Continue to volunteer for community programs and stay in touch with past coaches. Skim the requirements for job postings at the NCAA Web site. What do colleges and universities want out of their potential hires?

Gain experience. Study hard. Give more than you expect to get back. Build a network. And don't be above taking the lowest of jobs on your way to a coaching career. With each position, you can move closer to your goal.

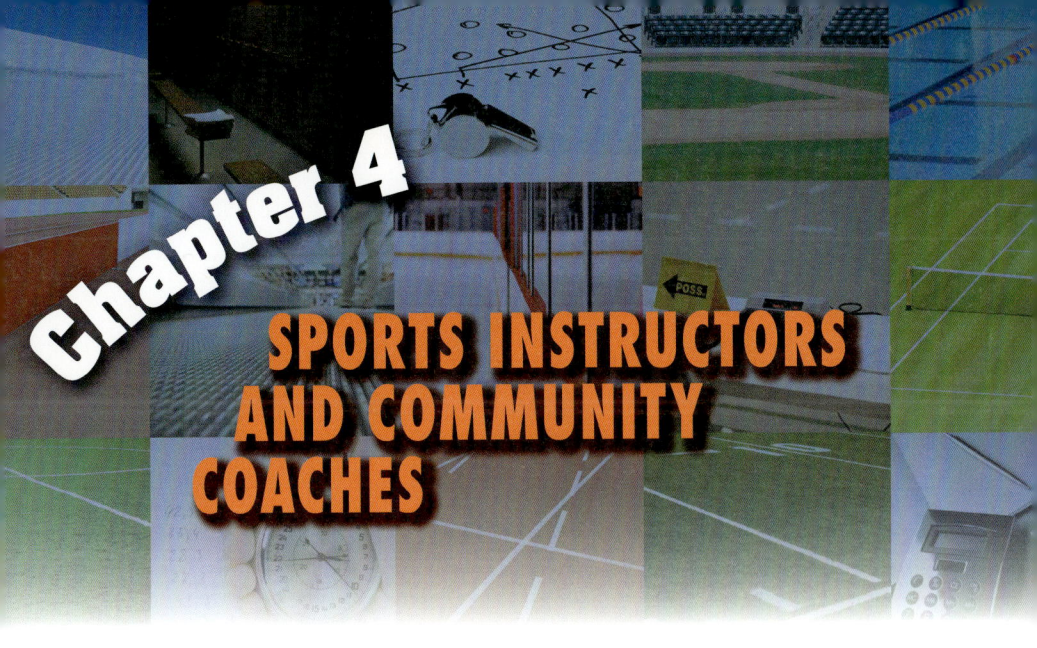

Chapter 4
SPORTS INSTRUCTORS AND COMMUNITY COACHES

Once upon a time, children learned how to finger a knuckleball or the fine art of the pass fake in neighborhood backyards and grade school playgrounds. It was a low-key way to learn the secret ways of sports. These skills were then honed for a few years before moving on to team tryouts and competitive leagues.

Times change. Spontaneous neighborhood pickup games of kickball or soccer aren't as easy to find as they were thirty years ago. Families are smaller. Weekdays are increasingly structured around after school care and summer camps. Television and computers keep people tethered inside. Fewer middle schools offer broad choices for intramural sports programs.

Study after study shows the positive impact athletic activities have on children: higher self-esteem and self-confidence and lower cases of childhood obesity. Early emphasis on physical fitness sets a foundation for healthy

Dream Jobs in Coaching

Country clubs and community parks and recreation departments rely on good coaches. Coaches need to be teachers and love their sport. These coaches often give youngsters their first exposure to sports and athletics.

SPORTS INSTRUCTORS AND COMMUNITY COACHES

lifestyle choices as the child becomes an adult. Children who play sports taught by responsible, thoughtful coaches tend to have better grades and are less likely to engage in dangerous behavior.

For many youngsters nowadays, their first introduction to playing sports comes from community and youth programs offered through parks and recreation departments or local groups like the YMCA. Often, the coaches are volunteers, such as parents or high school and college students interested in coaching. But some places, such as country clubs, private athletic or health clubs, and a few parks and recreation departments maintain a staff of pros—instructors who are available to teach small groups or one-on-one classes.

These jobs aren't necessarily coaching for competition, although private clubs will often act as home base for a team. Instructors may also act as coaches for these elite teams. For the most part, these coaches and instructors teach the fundamental skills of a sport, such as how to hold a tennis racket, balance on a beam, or swing a golf club. At the beginning level, an instructor or coach may set up scrimmages or games, but often there is no ranking involved, no push for the ultimate trophy or medal. Everyone gets to bat, regardless of strikes or outs. Everyone gets to dribble the ball or go for a goal. Everyone takes turns sitting out so that another can play. Sometimes scores aren't even kept.

Dream Jobs in Coaching

COACHES' SPOTLIGHT: JENIFER WOOD, YOUTH SOCCER, WEST VALLEY CITY, UTAH

It's hard to find time and space to add too much more into a life already filled with four young sons. But Jenifer Wood thought soccer would be the perfect sport for her active boys. They'd run around in the fresh air. They'd learn about teamwork. So Wood made time to volunteer as her oldest son's coach.

The following year she took on coaching duties for her second son. And in 2010, her third year of coaching, she added her third son's team to her coaching duties. Wood also took on a special mantel. U.S. Youth Soccer named her one of its two Recreational Coaches of the Year. The award honors coaches who exemplify the values of good sportsmanship, player development, personal coaching development, and community involvement.

The parents and players who work with Wood say she creates a practice and game day environment where children and parents have fun and learn. In accepting her award, Wood tried to duck out of the spotlight. She wanted to shine it on all volunteer coaches who give so much of their time so young children can have a great experience playing sports.

Community youth programs offer skill-based learning teams and competitive teams that focus on increasing knowledge and skill. So many programs rely on volunteer coaches. The best coaches teach the game, but more important, they model sportsmanship and leadership—and their actions influence the children they coach. Yet another team of young athletes will benefit from Wood's volunteer coaching. She took on her fourth son's team in 2011.

As the levels progress, score keeping and rankings come into play. Playoff games may be scheduled to more fairly rank teams within a league. For the most part, however, coaches remain focused on teaching the next set of skills and gradually introducing strategy concepts.

Many parks and recreation programs offer a complete menu of athletics geared toward younger children. These beginners come into a sport with varied skill levels. Some may be naturally gifted and intuitive. Some may not yet know how to share the ball or the spotlight. Some prefer to chase a butterfly or draw circles in the dirt.

Sometimes parks and recreation departments offer a few beginner classes for adults, too. Most private clubs will offer beginner classes for older children, teens, and adults. These athletes don't foster dreams of going pro. They just want to learn how to play a game they enjoy, possibly make a school team, or have friendly competitions. At this stage a coach's main role is to teach the fundamentals while making it fun.

A COACH'S UNIQUE ROLE IN EARLY CHILDHOOD

Some young children at a higher level of athletic ability and drive may thrive in a competitive team, but the majority needs to learn the basics and then some. Mostly they and their parents want to have fun at this age. The key as a coach is to recognize the individual players' abilities and his or her own expectations.

Do you demand drive, determination, and effort that creates wins? Do mistakes make you cringe in frustration? Coaching a beginner skills class may not be for you. Do you want to share your love of a sport? Do you like to focus on teamwork or helping an athlete to mentally focus on achieving personal bests? Do you want to help a child discover how moving an arm or leg differently can change how a ball responds? If so, then you may have found your niche.

That isn't to say you can't be both. You just need to recognize which side to show your athletes.

Take for example Kansas high school varsity football coach Tim Callaghan. In the Shawnee Mission West High School locker room he's an imposing figure who demands focus, teamwork, commitment, and flawless execution. In his first nine seasons as head coach, his Vikings earned multiple district champion titles and made the playoffs five times, including an appearance at the state championship game in 2006. The Vikings went undefeated in the 2008 regular season.

In 2010, Callaghan signed on as head coach for his son's third-grade tackle football team, which was organized through a local football and cheerleading club. Many boys had never played tackle before. At the first practice, Callaghan told players and parents, "I don't care if we lose every game. If each boy can block and tackle by the end of the season, then we've won."

Practice drills focused on tackling and blocking skills. Put hands here. Move feet this way. Get into a low stance like so for a clean, swift tackle. Every mistake was a learning opportunity. Here's what went wrong. Here's how to do it better next time.

Callaghan asked the boys to bring their spelling and math tests to practice so he could see if they were keeping up at school. He told them to study hard. He reminded them that they, not their parents, were responsible for their pads, helmets, and water bottles. He encouraged them to help around the house and play hard at recess.

Each boy running to and from the sideline got a pat on the shoulder. They gathered for a team cheer at the end of every practice and game.

His third graders didn't need a force intent on pushing them to championship-level performances. They

Dream Jobs in Coaching

COACHES' SPOTLIGHT: MELODY DAVIDSON, WOMEN'S HOCKEY, CANADA NATIONAL

Melody Davidson knows hockey. The head coach of the Canadian women's national hockey team has been a player, a peewee coach, and junior league coach. She helped found the Shooting Star Hockey School in 1993. She served as head coach for Connecticut College and the Division I Cornell University. She plays hockey. She scouts hockey players. She teaches hockey hopefuls.

Davidson graduated in 1986 from the University of Alberta with a degree in physical education. She

Team Canada head coach Melody Davidson motivates her team during practice for the 2010 Winter Olympics in Vancouver, Canada. Few hockey coaches have reached the successes this Canadian Olympic Hall of Famer has achieved.

SPORTS INSTRUCTORS AND COMMUNITY COACHES

enrolled in Calgary's National Coaching Institute in 1996 and has never looked back. As a coach or assistant coach in Canada, she's earned three gold Olympic medals, four gold and two silver World Championship medals, a World Championship silver medal for her under eighteen team, plus many more. In fact, reading the list of her many accomplishments can make a person dizzy. It goes on and on, with more honors and awards added each year.

Her expertise is sought out, and in 2010 Davidson sat on the panel at the World Hockey Summit to discuss the future of women's hockey. That same year she was named Coach of the Year by the Coaching Association of Canada. She was listed on the Canadian Association for the Advancement of Women and Sport Physical Activity's Most Influential list five years in a row.

Davidson is in the Alberta Sports Hall of Fame. She's a three-time recipient of the Petro-Canada Coaching Excellence Award. Coaches of Canada awarded her the 2010 Jack Donohue Coach of the Year Award while south of the border the U.S. Sports Academy honored her with the 2010 Vivian Stringer Coaching Award. In 2011, Davidson was inducted into the Canadian Olympic Hall of Fame.

didn't need someone yelling at them for missed blocks or dropped balls. They needed a teacher first and a football coach second.

That fall Callaghan's varsity Vikings finished their season as co-Sunflower League Champions. His third-grade

Vikings went 0–8, last place out of twelve teams. They scored their first and only touchdown in their final game.

But Callaghan was satisfied. All the boys had tackling basics down. All were closer to consistently making blocks. They were learning how to move and where to look, even if they were far from perfect. Three games into the 2011 tackle season, the now–fourth grade Vikings were 2-1.

Callaghan will yell at his big boys on Friday night if he thinks they've played sloppy ball. But come Saturday afternoon with his fourth graders, he's more focused on skills than scoreboards. Still, he will grin widely when his little guys jump up and down after a touchdown.

"They get better at blocking with each game," he said in an interview, chest swelling with pride. And that's the best part of all.

IS AN INSTRUCTOR JOB THE ONE FOR YOU?

Being an instructor, a volunteer coach, or a club pro may not seem as exciting as coaching Division I athletes, but these jobs can be the perfect scenario for the right person. Teen and college students interested in sports management or coaching competitive teams will find this pace perfect for honing their coaching skills. The stress levels are much lower. Some will say it's coaching at its purest—teaching for love of the sport and not prestige, money, or television rights.

SPORTS INSTRUCTORS AND COMMUNITY COACHES

Individual sports need coaches who can help athletes achieve the mental toughness to get through a game or match solely on their own athletic skills.

Becoming a certified coach is a great step. A certified coach has been trained in player safety, motivation, strategy, and communication. Professional coaching organizations and community colleges can lead you in the right direction toward a certification.

Coaches can make a career out of community leagues and country clubs, but many find they need a second, possibly full-time job. Still, it's a great way to build up skills and reputation. The network built through these experiences can lead to bigger opportunities in the future.

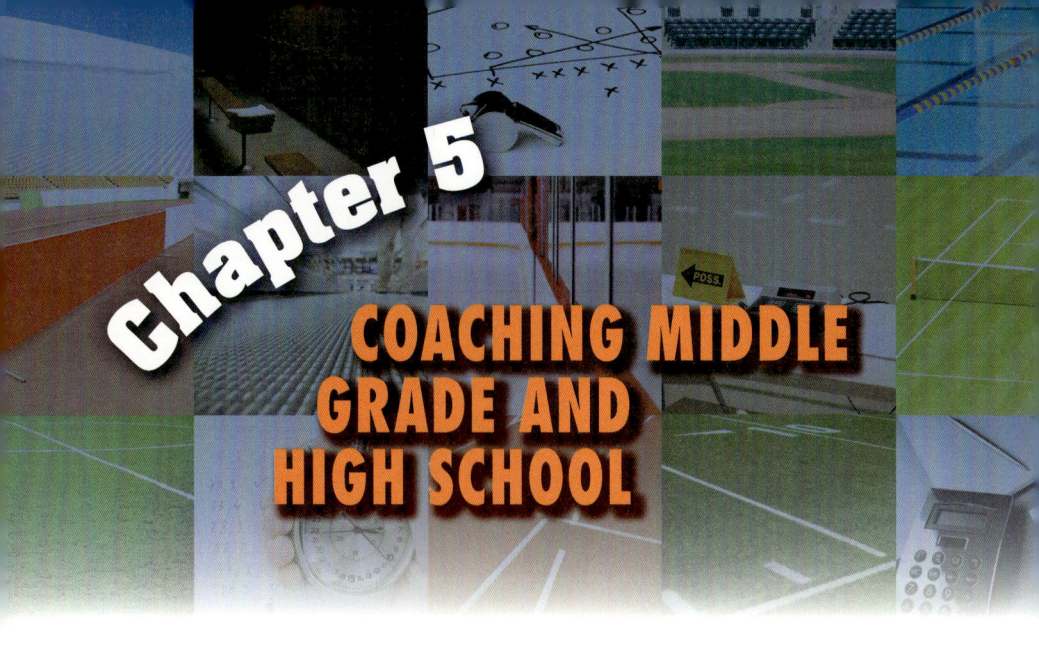

Chapter 5
COACHING MIDDLE GRADE AND HIGH SCHOOL

High school coaches play unique roles in this world. Only a small percentage of students will go on to play at the college level and even fewer professionally. A high school coach is often the most influential coach an athlete will have. Sometimes, a high school coach may be the only positive role model a student has in his or her life.

High school coaches touch more lives more deeply than any other coach. They might not coach more athletes than a college or professional coach, but they will serve as a guiding force for those many students whose athletic careers end at graduation. Those athletes might still play recreationally or even competitively, but they'll never have a coach spurring them on throughout the game like they had in high school.

It's truly a calling to coach at the high school or middle school level. The need for a teacher is still there, but the focus shifts from fundamentals and fun to strategy, motivation, and finding balance between academics and athletics.

COACHING MIDDLE GRADE AND HIGH SCHOOL

Middle-grade athletes go through more physical and emotional changes in a few short years than at any other time. Coaches need a strong understanding of physiology, anatomy, nutrition, and psychology.

High school coaches learn to recognize what individual athletes need to stay focused and driven to achieve. Team sport coaches need to build depth and create unified goals. They also need to be mindful of their role in character building. Student athletes look to their coaches to learn integrity, core values, and sportsmanship.

The best coaches don't give hollow praise. They also don't belittle. They expect performance from their athletes and can readily spot the difference between determination that falls short and lax efforts that lead to loss.

Perhaps the most important lesson a coach can teach at this level is how to keep an athlete's head in the game.

Narrow focus. What needs to be accomplished at this given moment in the game? Disregard the doubt. Disregard the opponent who uses mental games to build upon the smallest doubt. Shake off and learn from mistakes. Believe in accomplishment through determination and honest, relentless effort.

MIDDLE SCHOOLERS' UNIQUE NEEDS

Coaches who work with children between the ages of ten and fourteen reach these athletes at a critical time in their physical and emotional growth. For starters, their bones are growing like crazy. In fact, the bones grow so much faster than their muscles can develop. That causes the clumsy awkwardness of so many middle schoolers. Girls, of course, tend to reach their physical maturity sooner than boys.

Top this with the varied emotional states middle schoolers often find themselves in: increased self-consciousness, heightened sensitivity to criticism, and sometimes a pack mentality around their close friends. They tend to blow off their studies if it means a chance to spend more time with their peers. At the same time, they are idealistic and have a strong sense of justice.

What it comes down to is that coaches have a unique role to fill. The Association of Middle Level Education (AMLE) recommends that middle schools offer a variety of no-cut intramural sports. No-cut programs allow

COACHING MIDDLE GRADE AND HIGH SCHOOL

COACHES' SPOTLIGHT: JOHN MCKISSICK, FOOTBALL, SUMMERVILLE HIGH SCHOOL, SUMMERVILLE, SOUTH CAROLINA

One high school. Ten state titles. And 586 wins.

No typo. John McKissick, the varsity football coach for the Summerville Green Wave football team, can claim 586 winning games, the most for any football team that ever played, whether high school, college, or professional. He is also the first coach to hit the 500 mark.

Admirers say he didn't just teach football. They are right. When McKissick first took the job, he coached boys and girls basketball, baseball, and track. He also taught South Carolina history and U.S. history. And he mowed and lined the football field, shined the cleats, washed the uniforms, and taped ankles.

But that isn't what they mean. McKissick builds people. He builds community. And he builds pride in a town of less than thirty thousand residents. Nearly half show up to cheer each time his Green Wave team takes the field.

He knows what's important in life, they say, and it isn't winning at football.

Growing up poor during the Great Depression meant no shoes for school. No running water. Little to eat. That hard life forged McKissick's drive to achieve. It also fostered empathy for those struggling to achieve or lacking confidence to try. He tries to build them up.

He'll say working with kids has kept him young and made him a better person. The thousands of students he's coached in his fifty-seven years will say McKissick helped them grow up and taught them to be their best.

students to compete in a low-stress environment. It lets them experience good sportsmanship. It gives athletes a strong transition into their high school sports, even if they already play on a competitive team. It is also fun for those students who don't want the demands of playing for a school team.

CAREER PATH LIGHTS

If you think high school might be your calling, you're in luck. Coaching opportunities at middle and high schools are more readily available than at college or professional teams. This is a great starting point for aspiring coaches. Teens who aren't players but think they would like to coach can volunteer as equipment managers or student assistants to the coach. They can learn management and strategies to prepare for college.

Some college students coach high school teams while attending their own classes. Most public schools require state certification to coach. This is especially true of instructors in scuba, tennis, golf, karate, and so on. Certification usually means attending a class, being certified in CPR, passing a background check, and passing a test about responsible coaching.

Some elite private or parochial schools may have the means to hire coaches who coach only a given sport, but this isn't the case for the majority of schools. Even the largest high schools may expect coaches to pull double sport duties.

COACHING MIDDLE GRADE AND HIGH SCHOOL

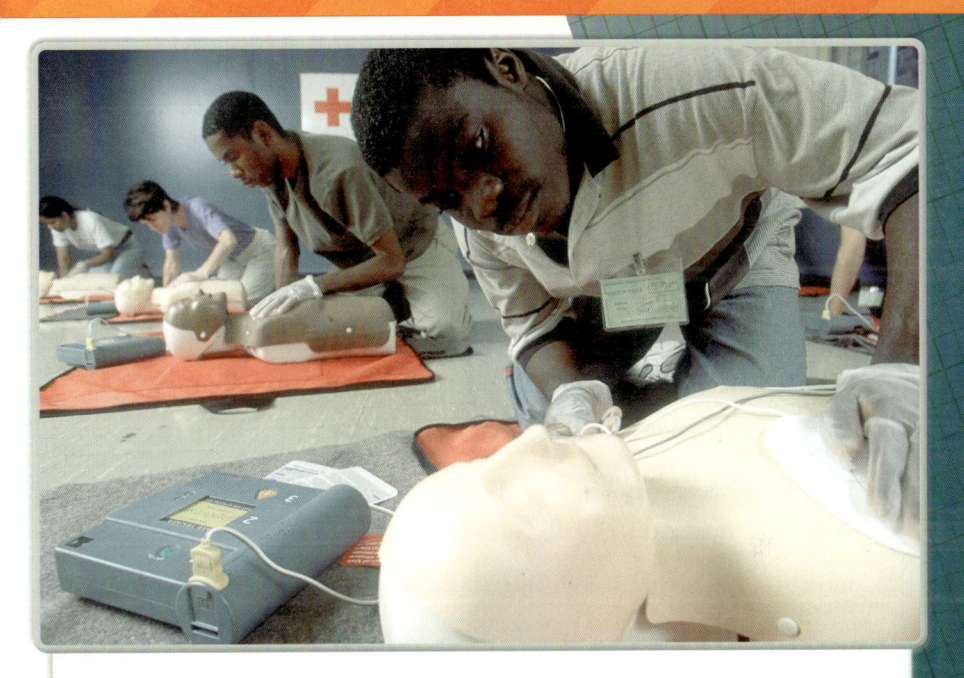

One of the smartest moves an aspiring coach can do is become a certified coach. These programs provide training in CPR, first aid, water rescue, ethics, and coaching techniques.

The realities of the modern economy mean that many school districts face budget cuts, decreased fund-raising opportunities, and streamlined staffs. For a person on the cusp of a coaching career, this means most schools want coaches who can also teach curriculum.

While physical education degrees make sense for someone who desires a coaching career, those with degrees in other subjects are just as in demand. A school can have only so many gym teachers. It may want a tennis coach who can teach American government, a volleyball coach comfortable in a biology lab, and a cross-country coach who can speak German.

Dream Jobs in Coaching

Then there's the travel factor. Many middle schools have dropped athletics because they can't afford an extra coach's salary. Some districts make it financially possible to keep certain programs in play by sharing teachers among two or more schools. This means a teacher/coach may take on triple roles: coaching track at the middle school and high school plus serving as a high school curriculum teacher. Some teachers might commute between classrooms in a high school and a middle school, only to coach at a third school. Any flexibility a potential coach can bring to the hiring table is a bonus.

What's more, high school coaching staffs tend to be small. Even in Texas, the setting for the television drama and major motion picture *Friday Night Lights*, all but the most celebrated head coaches play many roles. For example, the Texas 5A state champion Trinity High School in Euless, Texas, has eleven football coaches. One assistant coach teaches English and is also head baseball coach. Another assistant football coach is the track head coach, while the varsity defensive coordinator serves as his assistant.

Because of its size and the unique skill requirements of different positions, a high school football team might have up to a dozen individual coaches: head coach, offensive coordinator, quarterback coach, defensive coordinator, running backs coach, receiver coach, linebacker coach, and so on. Those assistant coaches likely

COACHING MIDDLE GRADE AND HIGH SCHOOL

also coach the freshman, sophomore, or junior varsity football teams.

Other sports, however, have much shallower coaching pools. There might be a head coach with one assistant, or in some cases a head coach and student managers. Some schools might not have enough students to warrant a wide variety of sports and so opt out of offering a less popular sport for that geographical area. You won't find a ski team at a Nebraska school, no matter how many students like to hit the slopes.

The dramas found on and off of Texas's high school football fields inspired sports journalist H. G. Bissinger to write the nonfiction book *Friday Night Lights*. It later became a movie and television series.

Building a coaching career is part athletic ability, part desire to teach, part passion and drive, and part networking. Students who play sports throughout their high school years and want to coach might find it easier to get a job at their former high school or in their former school district. They know the coaches. They know the approach to the game. With an education degree and teacher certification, they can get on staff coaching part-time and start building their coaching career.

Dream Jobs in Coaching

COACHES' SPOTLIGHT: NATALIE ROSEN, FOOTBALL, CALVIN COOLIDGE SENIOR HIGH, WASHINGTON, D.C.

In March 2010, Natalie Rosen stepped before a crowd of flashing cameras and microphone-wielding reporters to announce she was the new head coach for the Calvin Coolidge Senior High School varsity football team.

She isn't the first woman hired to coach football. Famed kicking coach Carol White was the trailblazer back in 1970. Two years before Title IX, the then-librarian found herself unexpectedly helping out the struggling Monroe High School in Albany, Georgia.

What makes Rosen unique is that she probably is the only female varsity football coach who knows exactly what it's like to play full-contact professional football. Rosen spent five years as wide receiver for the Independent Women's Football League's D.C. Divas. She knows the crunch, the pain, the risk of injury, the mental toughness a player needs each time he—or she—takes the field.

The media frenzy that was Coolidge High's opening game dwindled to nearly nothing before the Colts earned their first win under Rosen's guidance. Coolidge's 2010 football season ended 6-4, still admirable considering one of the team's leading players transferred to another school early in the season. But Rosen's successes off the field are the qualities that make her an excellent and inspiring coach. Rosen enforces mandatory study halls and SAT practice tests to help her players find success in the classroom as well as the gridiron.

NATIONAL HIGH SCHOOL ATHLETIC COACHES ASSOCIATION

The National High School Athletic Coaches Association (NHSACA) knows that high school coaches are role models to all youth and critical links to students who have little more than sports in their lives. The association works to train current and future coaches, giving them the tools and support they need. Coaches can get legal advice. They can earn college credit through programs in coaching leadership, as well as those that cover specific sports, drug abuse prevention, and concussion evaluation.

The strength and conditioning center offers training videos to help athletic directors and coaches properly and safely train their players. The nutrition center provides sport-specific nutritional information and training tips. Its Web site offers helpful links to state coaches associations as well as such topics as "Athletes for a Better World" and "Positive Coaching Alliance," and information about Title IX. NHSACA members can get discounts on equipment purchases through the organization's online store.

Each year the organization recognizes those outstanding coaches who do so much for their players. The Coach of the Year Awards shine the "National Spotlight" on about 160 coaches each year at the annual NHSACA conference in June.

Chapter 6
COACHING AT THE COLLEGIATE LEVEL

Turn on the television or computer and you'll likely stumble upon a story about yet another sports star landing a seven-figure deal. Those tales are so common that fans hardly blink anymore.

But what if that sports star with the million-plus contract offer happened to be a coach? A collegiate coach at that? Seven figures, all before factoring in sweet extras like a $3 million retention bonus if he's still around in five years?

Believe it or not, at least thirty-two Division I basketball coaches and more than fifty football coaches earned over $1 million in 2011. Topping the list: Alabama Crimson Tide football coach Nick Saban, who earns almost $6 million. University of Texas coach Mack Brown holds second place at more than $5.1 million, while Oklahoma Sooners coach Bob Stoops comes in third with almost $4.4 million.

COACHING AT THE COLLEGIATE LEVEL

Superstar quarterback Peyton Manning wasn't born with a shotgun arm and an uncanny ability to read a defense. He worked for years with coaches: first his father, then many coaches in high school, college, and the pros.

Back on the basketball court, Kentucky's John Calipari earns a base pay of $4 million, but there's a $3 million retention bonus waiting for him if he lasts five years. Michigan's Tom Izzo rounds out the top three, raking in $3.4 million.

Are these coaches worth that much dough? Whether or not anyone else thinks so, the fact remains that elite coaches are the face of their teams. Their reputations draw the top talent. Their records lure in the big donors. Standout players might be stars for a season or more, but they play for a maximum of four years before moving on.

And it's true that head coaches work long, hard hours under stressful, demanding conditions to deliver. It's more than designing plays or a full-court press. They are right there at every practice, correcting technique, pointing out weaknesses or errors. They assess the upcoming opponents and calculate how to take advantage of any weakness. They are gone from home for long stretches at a time.

Coaches manage their assistant coaches. They work to ensure each player remains in top condition and gets essential nutrients for a healthy body and mind.

And that's just what they do for the game. Add in interviews with magazines, radio, and television. Don't forget schmoozing with sponsors and alumni at fundraisers and university-sponsored events. Then comes the recruiting—the part of the job that takes up as much or more time than the regular season and causes the most

COACHING AT THE COLLEGIATE LEVEL

COACHES' SPOTLIGHT: DON MEYER, MEN'S BASKETBALL, NORTHERN STATE UNIVERSITY

In July 2009, NCAA varsity men's basketball coach Don Meyer was honored with the Jimmy V. Perseverance Award. The award was especially poignant after a brutal year.

While leading his Northern State University Wolves down the highway to a retreat in September 2008, Meyer fell asleep at the wheel. He was alone. The players driving behind him watched, helpless, as Meyer's Toyota Prius collided with a truck hauling 90,000 pounds (40,823 kilograms) of grain.

His fierce coaching style probably saved his life. As one player called 911, two climbed into the crushed Prius to care for Meyer. Others helped the stunned but uninjured truck driver and directed traffic until first responders arrived a half hour later. When Meyer insisted on going to sleep at one point, his players did what Meyer had done to them so many times. They yelled at him to focus.

They didn't know that Meyer had damaged his spleen, his diaphragm had detached from his rib cage, and his left leg was shattered. They didn't see blood from a severed artery pooling in the blackness under the steering wheel. But their yells angered Meyer enough to stay awake.

After fighting to survive the night, he woke up to learn surgeons had found slow-growing carcinoid tumors in his liver and intestines. Three weeks later doctors amputated much of his left leg.

Dream Jobs in Coaching

Meyer pushed himself as hard as his players. Keep dancin'. Stay ahead of the pain. Do the next right thing.

He returned in time to complete the 2008–2009 season, maneuvering his wheelchair on the sidelines. A prosthetic leg gave him better mobility, but Meyer was increasingly frustrated that he couldn't demonstrate proper moves or correct technique. Unable to coach at his own demanding level, Don Meyer stepped down in 2010. He left a legacy that includes 923 overall wins, the most for any NCAA men's basketball coach.

stress. Films to watch. Camps to plan. More travel to woo the top prospects and make sure the recruitment process falls within NCAA rules.

Coaches dole out discipline when needed, and they accept full responsibility when things don't go well. The proverbial buck stops with them.

Seven figures are enough to make anyone yearn for the apex of sports coaching. The problem with conquering any mountain is that not many can stand at the tip-top at the same time. Those who stop to camp out below the tree line find there's a lot more room to stretch.

HYPERCOMPETITION

Available coaching jobs at the collegiate level are slim, especially those in Division I schools, but they do pop

COACHING AT THE COLLEGIATE LEVEL

Nick Saban started his career as an assistant at Kent State. He honed his chops as secondary and defensive coordinator in the NFL and was the Miami Dolphins head coach for a year before rolling into Alabama in 2007.

up now and again. It may take years, even decades, to be anywhere near the top of that mountain. The plus side to college teams is that they have a wide variety of sports, both team and individual athletics. Smaller colleges and community colleges might have fewer sports but opportunities open up faster as coaches use them for springboards to bigger schools.

Consider the types of jobs available at a top university's athletic department. The head honcho, of course, is the director of athletic services, followed by assistant athletic director and associate athletic directors. There are

Dream Jobs in Coaching

many administrative jobs covering operations, facilities, and so on. Among coaches you'll find strength and conditioning coaches within each sport, directors of operation, assistant coaches, graduate assistant positions, equipment managers, even team trainers. There are jobs in the business office, public relations, student relations, individual sport contacts, financial aid, conference contact, sport development, training rooms, sports medicine, and so on.

Now look at the coaching staffs. The actual numbers are about the same as at high school—eleven football

Colleges offer a broader range of athletics, including swimming, which means more coaching jobs than any other school, community program, or private club. Intern and student manager opportunities are a great way to make connections.

coaches and six basketball coaches. But a broader selection of other sports means potentially more coaching opportunities. While many high school sports have a head coach and one or two assistant coaches, if they are lucky, many colleges and universities staff six to eight for such sports as soccer, basketball, baseball, even tennis. Sports like volleyball, gymnastics, track, and swim and dive teams have four to six coaches.

Of course the actual number depends upon the size of the school. Smaller colleges and universities may have fewer coaching positions, especially as you move down the division ladder. And much like high school, those that are Division III and NAIA may find coaches pulling the same double duty as coaches in high school. They may coach two or more sports, serve as athletic directors, or teach.

It's true that coaches in the upper echelons of Division I sports—the football and basketball coaches in particular but other sports as well—can make a lucrative salary. Most college coaches, however, make salaries comparable to their teacher counterparts. If they're fortunate and proven and have been with the university a few years or more, perhaps they'll break six figures.

There are few Division I schools where a coach might strive to land and stay until retirement. Those schools can afford the big bucks it takes to lure the very best names and reputations in coaching.

Dream Jobs in Coaching

COACHES' SPOTLIGHT: PAT SUMMITT, WOMEN'S BASKETBALL, UNIVERSITY OF TENNESSEE

Pat Summitt is truly in the top tier of coaches. On February 5, 2009, Summitt became the first Division I basketball coach, men's or women's, to win one thousand games when her Tennessee Lady Volunteers defeated the Georgia Lady Bulldogs.

Summitt played basketball and volleyball at the University of Tennessee-Martin. She was a twenty-one-year-old senior recovering from a blown knee in 1974 when Tennessee's chairperson of the physical education department offered her two jobs: assistant coach and graduate teaching assistant. Two weeks later Summitt received a second call. The head coach had decided to take a sabbatical. The job was hers if she wanted.

Summitt led the Lady Vols to a 16–8 record that year, while simultaneously teaching and attending her own graduate classes. She took time off in 1975 to play on the U.S. Women's World Championship and the Pan American Games teams. She returned to Tennessee for the '75–'76 season, led her team to a second-place

Pat Summitt has been the Lady Volunteers head basketball coach since 1974. Every Lady Vol from 1976 to this book's publication has made it to at least one NCAA Final Four game.

tournament finish, and made the Olympic team as cocaptain. The 1976 U.S. women's basketball team took home the silver.

Her commitment to her teams is legendary. In 1990, a very pregnant Summitt went into labor while recruiting a player in Pennsylvania. Summitt finished their meeting and caught a plane home because, as she told the pilots, she wanted her son to be born in Tennessee.

Summitt was the 1987, 1989, 1994, 1998, and 2004 Naismith College Coach of the Year; the WBCA/Converse Coach of the Year in 1983 and 1995; and the IKON/WBCA Coach of the Year in 1998. In 1990, Summitt received the John Bunn Award from the Basketball Hall of Fame, the first woman to receive the prestigious award in the hall's history.

Two years after her historic thousandth win, fifty-nine-year-old Summitt announced her doctors had diagnosed early-onset Alzheimer's-type dementia. Despite these new challenges, she'll likely hold on to her title of winningest basketball coach for a while. Only Bobby Knight and Pat Conroy are within one hundred games of Summitt's record as of 2011. Both are retired.

WHAT DOES IT TAKE TO BREAK INTO A TOP DIVISION I SCHOOL?

For the most part, finding positions at the top schools involves lots of hard work and networking. Former players may return as graduate assistants and work their way up

Dream Jobs in Coaching

When deciding what degree to pursue, many hoping to build a coaching career choose physical education or sports management. But there is demand for coaches with varied degrees. Follow your passion.

to assistant coach. After studying at the heels of masters, they move on to smaller schools or perhaps take another assistant coaching job at a slightly higher-ranked school.

Most universities require at least a bachelor's degree. The smaller the school, the more likely it wants someone with a master's degree as well. This seems a backward statement—why would a smaller school that pays a lower salary want someone with better academic credentials? Why would someone with that level of degree take a lower-paying job?

It's the nature of the collegiate game. Smaller schools need flexible coaches who can play multiple roles. Smart coaches know that the experience they'll gain running a small athletic department and coaching an NAIA team will be invaluable for their futures. When the opportunity arises, you may find yourself on the short list for Division II schools that want the experience and talent you offer. In time, a Division I school may seek you out.

It's a smart career path: earn a degree in a subject you love. Seek out an assistant or low-level position at a university with a lower salary than you prefer. Work your tail off. Make connections. Earn a master's degree in sports management. Take an assistant coaching job at a smaller university. Work your tail off some more. Observe. Learn how to scout. Learn the art of recruiting. Take a head coaching job when opportunity presents itself. Build or maintain a successful program. Take chances. Grab onto the ladder and move up when you can.

Chapter 7
COACHING A PROFESSIONAL TEAM

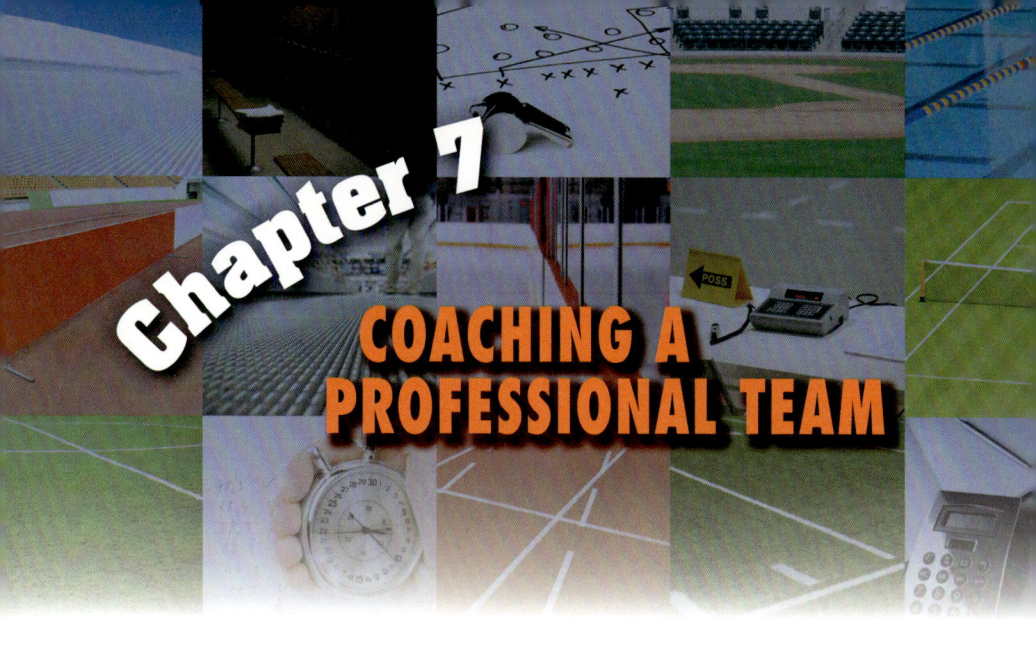

Like collegiate sports, professional teams emit an aura of glamour for aspiring coaches. Packed stadiums and auditoriums. Cheering crowds. Television rights. Hobnobbing with star athletes and sometimes star fans. Jet-setting around the globe, searching for future star players.

The professional field is even narrower than Division I collegiate sports. The best of the best athletes rise to this tier. The same goes for coaches. Of course in professional baseball, the head coach's official title is field manager. Still, the players refer to their manager as "coach." For this book's purposes, the term "head coach" includes field managers.

Ironically, many professional head coaches report base salaries that equal maybe half of what the top-paid Division I tournament coaches earn. In America for the most part, coaches aren't the stars in the pros like they are

COACHING A PROFESSIONAL TEAM

Mike Krzyzewski has led Duke to three NCAA championships, ten ACC tournament titles, and eleven regular season championships. Despite lucrative offers from several NBA teams, Coach K says he has no desire to leave Duke.

Dream Jobs in Coaching

at the collegiate level. Fans come for the athletes. Still, the bonuses and extras are lucrative.

Talented players might want to play for a certain coach, but ultimately the decision comes down to business. What will be best for the franchise? Coaches and players are, for the most part, business assets that can be liquidated or traded if it means a stronger bottom line.

Coaching hopefuls wanting to rake in the big salary bucks will need to make it big in European football, or soccer. Luis Felipe Scolari earned a whopping eight figures for being the top dog in soccer.

Of course there are exceptions around the world, especially when it comes to football—European football, or soccer, that is. The highest-paid coach in the world in 2009 was Luiz Felipe Scolari, former coach of World Cup

COACHING A PROFESSIONAL TEAM

COACHES' SPOTLIGHT: TOM FLORES, FIRST HISPANIC NFL QUARTERBACK AND NFL COACH, OAKLAND RAIDERS

In 1960, the newly formed Oakland Raiders recruited a former quarterback from the University of the Pacific named Tom Flores. Flores had been cut by two teams the previous two years, but the fledging franchise was willing to take a chance. He played under the legendary Al Davis for six years in the 1960s before being traded to the Buffalo Bills and eventually the Kansas City Chiefs in 1969. Flores retired in 1970

But Oakland was in his blood, and in 1972 Flores returned to cut his coaching teeth on the leather of John Madden. As an assistant coach for wide receivers, tight ends, and quarterbacks, Flores focused on the passing game. The Oakland Raiders were a force, winning Super Bowl XI in 1976 and earning Flores his second ring.

In 1979 Madden retired, and Flores was named head coach. His wild card Raiders were Super Bowl champions for the 1980 season. Flores and Chicago Cubs legend Mike Ditka are the only two people in NFL history to win Super Bowls as players, assistant coaches, and head coaches.

When the Raiders moved to Los Angeles in 1982, Flores went with them, nabbing his second ring as coach for the 1983 season. Flores retired as head coach in 1988 and became president and general manager of the Seattle Seahawks. He served as the Seahawks' coach in 1992 for two more years before retiring. He can't get the Raiders out of his blood, however, and still provides game day commentary through KSFO radio.

champions Brazil and former manager of Chelsea Football Club. Scolari was offered a staggering $24 million salary to coach Bunyodkor, the Uzbekistan championship team, in 2010. In fact, the top three highest-earning coaches in the world at that time headed football clubs. Los Angeles Lakers basketball head coach Phil Jackson nudged into fourth place with $10.3 million, just ahead of Manchester United's soccer coach Sir Alex Ferguson and his $10.2 million salary.

Five more European football coaches rounded out the top ten. American coaches didn't make another appearance on the list until Phoenix Suns coach Mike D'Antoni showed up at number twelve.

So yes, the odds of becoming a star coach and earning seven-figure salaries is slim at best. Another downside: professional coaches can be fired without a specific reason if the front office thinks that's the best move for the franchise. College coaches typically have a termination clause in their contracts that outlines specific reasons to be fired.

On the plus side, some professional coaching staffs are huge compared to colleges and high schools. Football teams might have seventeen coaches. A professional hockey team might have a coaching staff of ten. There are strength-training coaches, special teams coaches, one or two coaches for specific positions, a pool of assistant coaches, equipment managers, trainers, even massage therapists. Administrative jobs with a general manager or public relations roles can teach an aspiring coach the business side of professional sports as well. Opportunities to make the majors are there, even if the chances of settling in at the top seem next to impossible.

MORE TO PROFESSIONAL SPORTS THAN THE MAJORS

The big leagues aren't the only places to build a coaching career. Canadian leagues, European leagues, and minor and independent leagues all need excellent head and assistant coaches. True, some minor league coaches may find they need a second job to supplement their income. But the autonomy and freedom from franchise politics comes with its own rewards.

Take Hal Lanier for example. The Major League Baseball manager was fired during his third season with the Houston Astros after a tough six-game loss to the New York Mets. His stats in those three seasons included a National League West division title, a 96-win regular season, and a win-loss record of 22 games above .500. Pretty good, wouldn't you think?

No offers came his way for a year before the St. Louis Cardinals picked him up as bench coach in 1990. He was there for two seasons until the manager who hired him was fired. Lanier wasn't invited to return, either.

Years passed with no coach or manager offers for the big league. In 1996, Lanier accepted a job as manager for

Dream Jobs in Coaching

At the Corn Crib baseball field in Normal, Illinois, Cornbelters general manager Hal Lanier works third base. The former Major League Baseball coach has found a prolonged career in the independent baseball leagues.

an independent Northern League team in Winnipeg, Canada. Lanier has worked steadily ever since.

At this level, there is still need for a teacher, Lanier says, and that's the part he cherishes most. Even though he's the manager, he works the third-base coaching duties. He takes care of his team and fellow coaches, all while traveling around the continent playing the sport he loves. In sixteen seasons as an independent, Lanier has sent 150 of his players to affiliated minor league teams. Five even made it to the Big Show.

A DAY IN THE LIFE OF BIG-NAME SPORTS

A coach for a professional team plays the same role that a high school or collegiate coach plays, but with a few distinct differences. Professional coaches expect players to know what they're doing. A player might not know a new coach's unique strategy and approach to play, but the fundamentals should be so down pat that it's rote.

COACHING A PROFESSIONAL TEAM

COACHES' SPOTLIGHT: THE INIMITABLE YOGI BERRA, MAJOR LEAGUE BASEBALL

He's known for his Yogi-isms—misspoken words of wisdom, such as "It ain't over till it's over," "It's like déjà vu all over again," "We made a lot of wrong mistakes," and "When you come to a fork in the road, take it."

But Lawrence Peter "Yogi" Berra remains a beloved coach and an icon of baseball's golden age. Nicknamed for his resemblance to a snake charmer from a movie, Berra was only seventeen when he signed with the Yankees for $500 in 1942. He drove in a whopping twenty-three runs in one day of double-header play. Berra left

Yogi Berra spent much of his career in a New York Yankees uniform. He played for twenty years and coached off and on for another decade before landing in Houston.

Dream Jobs in Coaching

baseball the following year to join the U.S. Navy.

He played for a few farm teams after he returned, eventually making it to the majors in 1946. As a player, Berra was a fifteen-time All-Star and three-time Most Valuable Player (MVP) player, and played in fourteen World Series.

He was named Yankees manager in 1964 and led the team to the American League pennant that year. He was fired after losing to the Cardinals but rebounded by signing on as a player-coach for the New York Mets. He became manager in 1972 and coached the last-place team to a National League pennant the following year.

He left the Mets in 1975 and returned to the Yankees as coach a year later. In 1984 George Steinbrenner hired Berra as manager but replaced him just twenty-two games into the 1985 season. Yogi moved on to coach the Houston Astros, where he remained until he retired in 1992. He was inducted into the National Baseball Hall of Fame in 1972.

Missed blocks or blown shots aren't tolerated. Enough mistakes and a player will be shown the door before the season is over.

At the professional level, a coach can focus on the parts of the job he or she loves the most. Most leave the hands-on instruction to the deep team of assistant coaches. One coach might love to design plays. Another might prefer to pass that task on to an assistant and

COACHING A PROFESSIONAL TEAM

For some coaches, the best part of the job happens at that point in the game when it comes down to the next play. They must rely on their experience, their intuition, and the skills of their players to win.

focus the most effort and time on team development. One might want that hands-on interaction with players and pass the scouting and administration tasks to a trusted assistant coach.

All coaches are involved in recruiting and team development, but often the initial whittling is done by designated scouts. Typically the team's general manager and player's agent negotiate salaries and bonuses while the

Dream Jobs in Coaching

Ryne Sandberg is one of several former professional athletes who moved on to coaching. The Hall of Famer played for sixteen years before retiring in 1997. He now coaches rising stars in the minor leagues.

coach and player stay out of it. This is better for both. It keeps money out of their relationships. Together they can focus on athletic performance and team building instead.

Coaches also play a huge role in building community relations. They often are active in local charities and encourage their players to do the same. They give back to the fans as thanks for all the community gives them.

A DAY IN THE MINOR LEAGUE

A minor or independent league manager may also act as coach. At the same time, position coaches might also be players. They often act as their own scouts. They may be teaching young players on their way up to the majors or former major leaguers who aren't quite ready to leave the game. Teams affiliated with the majors may need to be accountable to the home team, but there is still a level of autonomy and independence not always found in the big leagues. It offers the best of both worlds: a chance to really coach and see a player soar without the pressures that come with big college or pro responsibilities.

Chapter 8
COACHING INDIVIDUAL SPORTS

Coaching athletes who compete in individual sports requires a completely different approach and mindset. Team sports need a certain amount of gung ho, which means an attitude of many working as one. Mentally and physically they strive for the same goal and learn to focus on the job at hand. But individual sports require coaching skills that focus even more on mental and physical endurance.

Think about the sports in which an individual competes alone. Gymnastics. Golf. Tennis. Swimming. Diving. Individual track and field. Cross country. Equestrian sports. Speed skating. Then there are the direct contact sports, such as fencing, wrestling, and karate. The athlete must overcome an opponent through strategy and skill without help from anyone else.

The list can go on and on. All need coaches to teach skills and motivate performance.

COACHING INDIVIDUAL SPORTS

Athletes in individual sports can't always rely on teammates to bolster motivation or help them find another burst of strength when exhaustion sets in. Many rely on their coaches to get them through difficult competitions.

While some schools offer individual sport programs, many young skeleton racers or Alpine skiers won't find their sport listed among their school's athletic departments. Community clubs—often coached by volunteer parents or part-time college students—are their first exposure to sports like ice skating, archery, and others.

At the high school level, many individual sports are considered no-cut programs. Anyone can join and play, regardless of performance. Much like coaches at the peewee level, individual sport coaches must learn to accommodate motivations and talents that run the gamut from "My mom forced me to sign up because she says I need to be more involved in the high school experience" to "If I push just a little harder I can top my personal best. Again."

THE UNIQUE APPROACH TO COACHING THE INDIVIDUAL

The coaching goals for physical performance are the same for individual sports as team sports: hone skills for graceful coordination. Condition the heart and lungs for endurance. Push nutrition and muscles for power and speed.

The approach to coaching for growth is also somewhat similar: find out an athlete's strengths and shortcomings. But ultimately a game's outcome depends upon the one. In individual sports, a coach can't substitute another

COACHING INDIVIDUAL SPORTS

COACHES' SPOTLIGHT: BELA KAROLYI, GYMNASTICS MAESTRO

Nadia Comaneci. Mary Lou Retton. Kim Zmeskal. Julianne McNamara. Phoebe Mills. Kerri Strug. Betty Okino. Dominique Moceanu.

These Olympic and world champions were coached by Bela Karolyi. Considered the most successful gymnastics coach ever, he can count among his students twenty-eight Olympians, nine Olympic champions, fifteen world champions, twelve European medalists, and six U.S. national champions.

Karolyi has coached gymnastics for more than thirty years. His breakout pupil was Nadia Comaneci, who

As a coach, Bela Karolyi demanded discipline and fire from his athletes. His focus on finding younger athletes, who had more range of motion, helped change the nature of modern gymnastics.

Dream Jobs in Coaching

wowed judges in the 1976 Olympics with her flawless execution. He was the Romania national coach back then. The duo repeated their golden efforts in the 1980 Olympics, but Karolyi and his wife, also a gymnastics coach, yearned to leave the oppression of Soviet-era Romania. The couple defected to the United States while on an exhibition tour in 1981.

It didn't take long before Karolyi was coaching Olympic hopefuls. Ten years after he defected, his women's gymnastics team won the silver medal at the World Championships, their first ever at that level. The team shone again in the 1992 Olympics in Barcelona, capturing a team bronze medal, the first in more than forty years for a nonboycotted Olympics. He tried to retire in 1992, but former student Kim Zmeskal persuaded him to train her for a comeback at the 1996 Olympics. Zmeskal, Dominique Moceanu, Kerri Strug, and the rest of their team won the team gold as well as many individual medals.

In 1990, Karolyi became the women's national team coordinator for USA Gymnastics and served for two years. Ten years after he tried to retire the first time, he retired again. His wife, Martha, took over as team coordinator. Their 500-acre (2 square km) Houston ranch is home to a gymnastics summer training camp.

player if the first needs a breather, or has an off day, or gets knocked around by an opponent, or loses focus.

For the athlete dependent upon nobody but him- or herself, concentration, confidence, and control become even more crucial to personal success. What's more, the solo athlete must dig deep down to find the motivation to go on when pinned down by an opponent or struggling in fourth place with a five-point deficit.

Coaches play a unique role. They, of course, are teachers. They demonstrate technique. They drill exercises designed to create muscle memory. The formulate strategy and assess the strengths and weaknesses of upcoming opponents.

But coaches also become a touchstone for the athlete. They are the source of strength when an ice skater doesn't want to try that double Salchow one more time because she knows she's going to fall on the cold, hard ice, and it hurts. They are a pair of eyes that a wrestler searches for in the crowd when he can't find the strength to wriggle out of a pin and the count keeps coming. They are a nod, a reminder that an athlete can find strength if he or she digs a little deeper. They are a voice in the head, saying "You can do it. You know how. It's all there."

Perhaps the most important lesson a coach can teach, whether to individual sport athletes or team players, is the ability to concentrate. The words are called out on every sideline.

Focus.

This ability helps instill in the athlete a sense of control. With control comes confidence. With confidence comes motivation.

Dream Jobs in Coaching

COACHES' SPOTLIGHT: JIM TATE, TRACK AND FIELD, ST. PAUL'S EPISCOPAL SCHOOL, MOBILE, ALABAMA

From 1983 to 1998, the same girls' cross country team captured the Alabama state championships each year. St. Paul's Episcopal School, led by coach Jim Tate, still holds the national record for most consecutive state championships in the nation. Altogether, Tate has led the girls to eighteen titles.

But those aren't the only awards his teams have earned. Since Tate started coaching track and field at St. Paul's in 1978, his boys have won thirteen outdoor track and field championships, eleven indoor titles, and nine cross-country crowns. The girls add another seventeen indoor crowns and twenty indoor titles to their eighteen championships. Add two crowns earned by his junior high teams, and Tate's athletes have won an impressive collection of awards. That's before the forty or so runner-up awards his teams can claim as well.

What makes this all the more meaningful is that Tate built the track and field program at St. Paul's from the ground up. More than fifty of his students have gone on to compete at the collegiate level.

It's quite a legacy for the soft-spoken Tate, who served in Vietnam from 1964 until 1969. When he returned stateside he was the athletic director and track and field coach for a few schools before starting the fledgling program at St. Paul's.

His athletes say he is a gentle leader who turns teenagers into champions, young men and women into leaders, and instills a spirit of sportsmanship, service, and honor.

COACHING INDIVIDUAL SPORTS

He has been inducted into the Mobile Sports Hall of Fame and the Alabama High School Athletic Association Hall of Fame. In 2010, the National High School Coaches Association named Tate the Girls Track and Field Coach of the Year.

IS THIS THE PATH FOR YOU?

Coaching individual sports can be immensely satisfying. Often country clubs, private athletic organizations, community centers, and other programs will retain coaches on staff. While one coach might teach several players, the best coaches go on to coach a limited number of elite athletes and sometimes may focus on just two or three.

Olympic teams require excellent coaches. Top college coaches will often serve as team coaches for the Olympics and world championships. For example, John Smith, head coach for Oklahoma State; Lou Rosselli, associate head coach at Ohio State; and Casey Cunningham, head assistant coach at Penn State, served on the coaching staff for the U.S. Freestyle World Team at the 2011 World Wrestling Championships in Istanbul, Turkey.

If you desire to coach individual athletics, you'll want to seek certification from an accredited organization. Most coaches, whether for team or individual sports, also

Dream Jobs in Coaching

As a wrestler, John Smith won six consecutive world championships and multiple Olympic gold medals. He uses those same skills to coach his Oklahoma State wrestlers to their own successes.

need to be certified and recertified in CPR and first aid. Coaches for water sports need to be certified in water rescue. They also need to pass background checks.

Classes about the psychology of motivation can help a coach better understand the dynamics behind athletic drive and mental fortitude. Physical education degrees as well as courses in anatomy, sports rehabilitation, and communication studies can build upon a future coach's natural instincts and abilities.

Check out the kinds of organizations and schools that offer the sport you'd like to coach. Ask other coaches lots of questions—what is the best part of working at a particular club or school? Ask the athletes what they want out of their sport.

The more you know now, the better prepared you are to chart a path. You'll know the direction you'd like to go and have a good idea of how to get to the finish line. Once you're on the path, it becomes a matter of enjoying every minute of the journey.

COLLEGE AND UNIVERSITY PROGRAMS IN COACHING AND PHYSICAL FITNESS

The following is a list of some colleges and universities that offer programs in coaching and physical fitness:

Adelphi University, Garden City, NY: Bachelor of science in physical education with a concentration in exercise science, including: sport skills enhancement, nutritional analysis, biomechanics, injury prevention, and personal training.

Belmont University, Nashville, TN: Majors in physical education and health; graduates have entered the fields of teaching, coaching, college athletics, and athletic and personal training.

Boston University, Boston, MA: Physical education, health education, and coaching programs.

Columbia University, New York, NY: coaching certification program, physical education.

Concordia University Irvine, Irvine, CA: Master of arts in coaching and athletic administration.

Georgetown University, Washington, D.C.: Degree in sports industry management.

Gonzaga University, Spokane, WA: Bachelor of education and physical education program; teacher certification in physical education.

Grand Canyon University, Phoenix, AZ: Bachelor of science in exercise science with an emphasis in athletic coaching.

Kent State University, Kent, OH: Athletic coaching certification.

United States Sports Academy, Daphne, AL:

COLLEGE AND UNIVERSITY PROGRAMS IN COACHING AND PHYSICAL FITNESS

Bachelor of sports science, master of sports science, doctor of education in sports management.

University of Georgia, Athens, GA: Bachelor degree in physical education, teaching, and coaching.

University of Kansas, Lawrence, KS: Bachelor degree in physical education, teaching, and coaching.

University of Nebraska, Lincoln, NE (Lincoln, Omaha, and Kearney): Bachelor degree in physical education, teaching, and coaching.

Valley City State University, Valley City, ND: Athletic coaching certification, degree in physical education.

Western Kentucky University, Bowling Green, KY: Master of science in athletic administration.

West Virginia University, Morgantown, WV: Bachelor of science in athletic coaching; master of science in athletic coaching education; master of science in physical education teacher education; master of science in sport management.

A CAREER IN COACHING AT A GLANCE

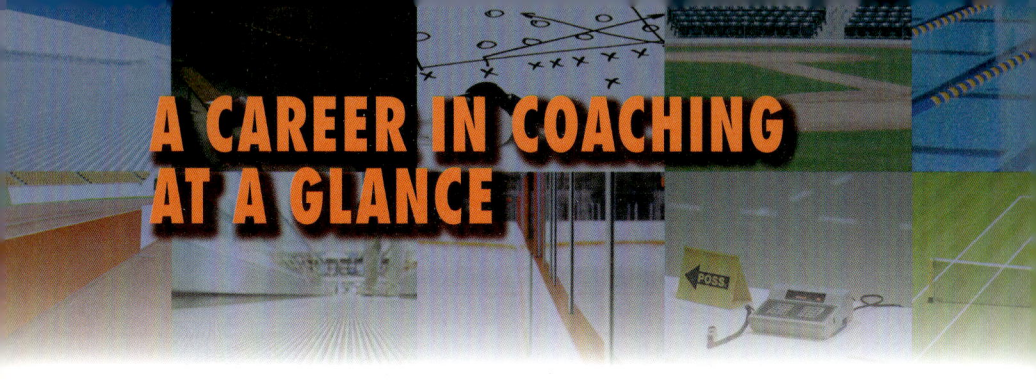

MIDDLE SCHOOL OR HIGH SCHOOL COACH
ACADEMICS

- Bachelor's degree
- Teacher certification

Experience

- Playing sports in middle school, high school, and college
- Volunteering as team manager
- Volunteering as assistant coach
- Coaching a children's team

Duties and Responsibilities

- Acting as mentor
- Advising players
- Organizing practices
- Traveling to games, making necessary arrangements
- Planning game strategies

A CAREER IN COACHING AT A GLANCE

COLLEGE COACH ACADEMICS

- Bachelor's degree
- Master's degree

Experience

- Playing sports in middle school, high school, and college
- Volunteering as team manager
- Volunteering as assistant coach
- Coaching a children's team

Duties and Responsibilities

- Acting as mentor
- Advising players
- Organizing practices
- Traveling to games, making necessary arrangements
- Planning game strategies
- Hiring assistant coaches
- Scouting new talent

PROFESSIONAL SPORTS COACH ACADEMICS

- Bachelor's degree
- Master's degree

Dream Jobs in Coaching

Experience

- Playing sports in middle school, high school, and college
- Volunteering as team manager
- Working as assistant coach.

Duties and Responsibilities

- Acting as mentor
- Advising players
- Organizing practices
- Traveling to games, making necessary arrangements
- Planning game strategies
- Hiring assistant coaches
- Meeting with the media for interviews
- Scouting new talent

BUREAU OF LABOR STATISTICS INFORMATION

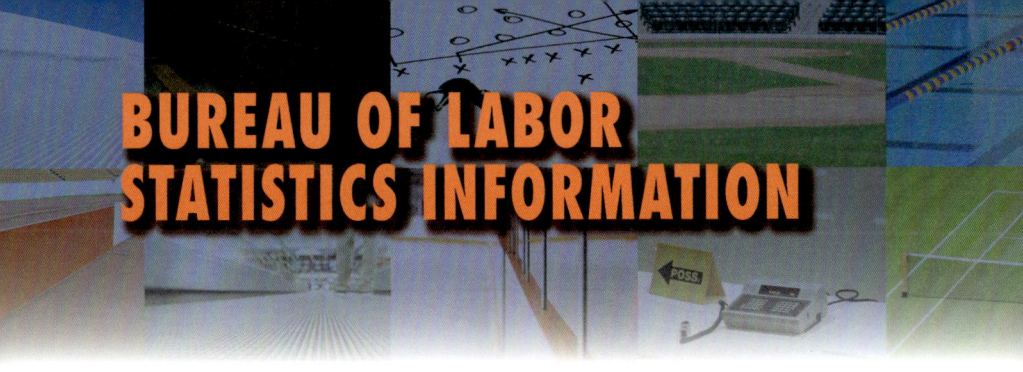

MIDDLE SCHOOL OR HIGH SCHOOL COACH

SIGNIFICANT POINTS

- Middle school and high school coaches work primarily as teachers.

- Teachers must hold a bachelor's degree in education, as well as pass a teacher certification program.

- Teachers and coaches must have the ability to communicate, inspire trust and confidence in students, and be able to motivate and be understanding of students' needs.

- Job prospects are best in high-demand areas, such as math, science, and language education.

NATURE OF THE WORK

Most high school and middle school coaches teach, in addition to coaching duties. Teachers foster the intellectual and social development of children during their formative years. They plan and assign lessons, administer and grade tests, listen to presentations, and maintain classroom discipline. Teachers also meet with parents to discuss students' progress.

TRAINING

The traditional route to becoming a public school teacher involves completing a bachelor's degree from a teacher education program and then obtaining a license. However, most states now offer alternative routes to licensure for those who have a college degree in other fields. Private school teachers do not have to be licensed but may still need a bachelor's degree.

OTHER QUALIFICATIONS

Teachers must have the ability to communicate, inspire trust and confidence, and motivate students, as well as understand the students' educational and emotional needs. Teachers must be able to recognize and respond to individual and cultural differences in students and employ different teaching methods that will result in higher student achievement. They should be organized, dependable, patient, and creative. Teachers also must be able to work cooperatively and communicate effectively with other teachers, support staff, parents, and members of the community.

ADVANCEMENT

Teachers may become administrators or supervisors. In some systems, highly qualified experienced teachers can become senior or mentor teachers, with higher pay and additional responsibilities. They guide and assist less experienced teachers while keeping most of their own teaching responsibilities.

JOB OUTLOOK

Job outlook will vary with the locality, grade level, and subject taught. Most job openings will result from the need to replace the large number of teachers who are expected to retire over the 2008–18 period. Also, many beginning teachers—especially those employed in poor, urban schools—decide to leave teaching for other careers after a year or two, creating additional job openings for teachers.

WORK ENVIRONMENT

Seeing students develop new skills and gain an appreciation of knowledge and learning can be very rewarding. Occasionally, teachers must cope with unruly behavior and violence in the schools. Teachers may experience stress in dealing with large classes, heavy workloads, or old schools that are run down and lack modern amenities. Accountability standards also may increase stress levels, with teachers expected to produce students who are able to exhibit a satisfactory performance on standardized tests in core subjects. Many teachers, particularly in public schools, also are frustrated by the lack of control they have over what they are required to teach.

COLLEGE OR PROFESSIONAL COACH

SIGNIFICANT POINTS

- These jobs require immense overall knowledge of the game, usually acquired through years of experience at lower levels.
- Fierce competition for jobs.

NATURE OF THE WORK

Coaches organize amateur and professional athletes and teach them the fundamental skills of individual and team sports. (In individual sports, instructors sometimes may fill this role.) Coaches train athletes for competition by holding practice sessions to perform drills that improve the athletes' form, technique, skills, and stamina. Along with refining athletes' individual skills, coaches are responsible for instilling good sportsmanship, a competitive spirit, and teamwork and for managing their teams during both practice sessions and competitions. Before competition, coaches evaluate or scout the opposing team to determine game strategies and practice specific plays. During competition, coaches may call specific plays intended to surprise or overpower the opponent, and they may substitute players for optimum team chemistry and success. Coaches' additional tasks may include selecting, storing, issuing, and taking inventory of equipment, materials, and supplies.

TRAINING

Most coaches get their training from having played in the sport at some level. All of these sports-related workers need to have an extensive knowledge of the way the sport is played, its rules and regulations, and strategies, which is often acquired by playing the sport in school or a recreation center but also with the help of instructors or coaches or in a camp that teaches the fundamentals of the sport.

OTHER QUALIFICATIONS

Coaches must relate well to others and possess good communication and leadership skills. They may need to pass a background check and applicable drug tests. Coaches must be resourceful and flexible to successfully instruct and motivate individuals and groups of athletes.

ADVANCEMENT

Many coaches begin their careers as assistant coaches to gain the knowledge and experience needed to become a head coach. Head coaches at large schools and colleges that strive to compete at the highest levels of a sport require substantial experience as a head coach at another school or as an assistant coach. To reach the ranks of professional coaching, a person usually needs years of coaching experience and a winning record in the lower ranks or experience as an athlete in that sport.

JOB OUTLOOK

Employment of coaches is expected to grow for all occupations through 2018. Very high competition is expected for jobs at the highest levels of sports with progressively more favorable opportunities in lower levels of competition.

WORK ENVIRONMENT

Irregular work hours are common for coaches. They often work Saturdays, Sundays, evenings, and holidays. Coaches usually work more than forty hours a week for several months during the sports season, if not most of the year. They may be exposed to all weather conditions of the season. Coaches frequently travel to sporting events.

GLOSSARY

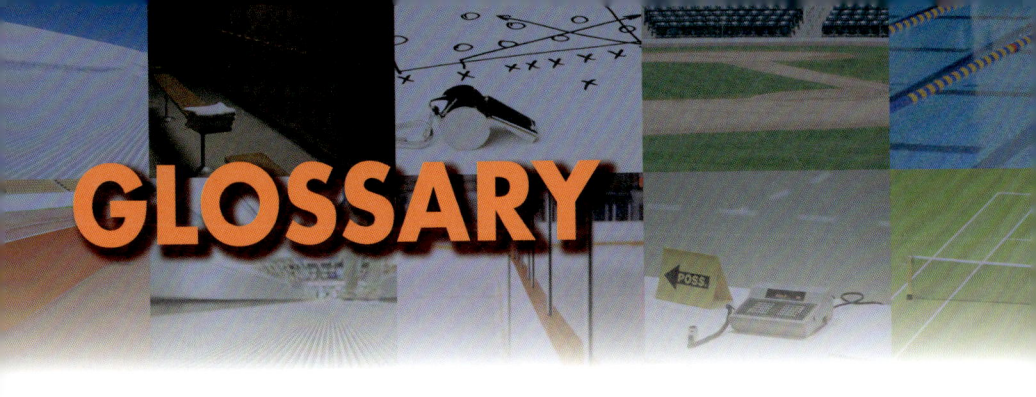

administration A sport's governing body.

affiliated team A minor league or farm team associated with a major league team.

athletic director The person who oversee all aspects of an athletic program, including hiring coaches, scheduling, budget preparation, promotion, and facility management.

burnout The point at which an athlete can no longer perform either physically or mentally.

cardiovascular Describing the body system that includes the heart and blood vessels.

certification The process of passing scrutiny to be considered an eligible, employable coach.

collegiate Having to do with a college or university and its students.

compulsory Required.

concussion A traumatic injury in which the brain is jostled or bruised.

conference A group of schools that join together to share athletic and academic competitions.

Division I Typically the major collegiate athletic power schools that offer fourteen athletic programs distributed fairly evenly between men's and women's sports.

European football Soccer. Football, as it's known in America, is often called American fooball, while soccer is called football around the world.

Dream Jobs in Coaching

field manager A head coach for major league baseball teams.

highlight reel A collection of an athlete's best moments on the court or field, which are shared with potential college recruiters.

independent league Professional sports teams that aren't affiliated with a major league team.

instructor Another name for a coach.

internal motivators The force that compels someone to succeed for his or her own satisfaction.

internship An opportunity to get on-the-job experience while still a student.

invitational A sports competition in which a specific group of athletes is invited to participate.

NAIA National Association of Intercollegiate Athletes.

NCAA National Collegiate Athletic Association.

network The process of meeting people who can benefit your future.

physiology The study of how living things function and move.

recruitment The process of asking a player to join a team.

salary cap A rule used in the National Football League to ensure team owners provide a level playing field for athletic competition.

scout A person who seeks out and makes connections with star athletes.

segregation The political and cultural separation of blacks and whites.

service learning program A program offered to sports administration students to teach them how to apply their newfound knowledge to humanitarian outreach programs.

GLOSSARY

sportsmanship The concept that players enjoy the game for the sake of the process and not to win or belittle opposing players.

strategy A plan designed to achieve a specific goal.

strength and conditioning The use of exercise and muscle building to enhance physical performance.

termination clause A legal description of when and why someone can be fired or released from an employment contract.

Title IX The United States law that barred gender discrimination in education, including athletics.

For More Information

Black Coaches and Administrators
Pan American Plaza
201 S. Capitol Avenue, Suite 495
Indianapolis, IN 46225
(317) 829-5600
Web site: http://www.bscasports.cstv.com
The Black Coaches and Administrators is a nonprofit organization dedicated to the growth and development of ethnic minorities at all levels of sports, both nationally and internationally. The group is comprised of coaches in professional sports, the NCAA, the NAIA, junior colleges, and high schools.

Lake Placid Winter Olympic Museum
2634 Main Street
Lake Placid, NY 12946
(518) 302-5377
Web site: http://www.whiteface.com/activities/museum.php
The Lake Placid Winter Olympic Museum calls itself the proverbial keeper of the flame. It tells the story of how this little mountain village twice became the center of

FOR MORE INFORMATION

the winter sports world when it hosted the Olympics in 1932 and 1980.

Naismith Memorial Basketball Hall of Fame
1000 West Columbus Avenue
Springfield, MA 01105-2518
(413) 781-6500
Web site: http://www.hoophall.com
Since 1959, the Naismith Memorial Basketball Hall of Fame has honored and celebrated the game's greatest moments and brightest stars. Hundreds of interactive exhibits share the spotlight with skills challenges, live clinics, and shooting contests.

National Association of Intercollegiate Athletics (NAIA)
1200 Grand Boulevard
Kansas City, MO 64106
(816) 595-8000
Web site: http://www.naia.org
The NAIA promotes the education and development of students through intercollegiate athletic participation. Member institutions believe participation in athletics serves as an integral part of the total education process.

National Baseball Hall of Fame
25 Main Street

Dream Jobs in Coaching

Cooperstown, NY 13326

(888) Hall-of-Fame (425-5633)

Web site: http://www.baseballhall.org

The National Baseball Hall of Fame and Museum is an independent, nonprofit educational institution. Through its many collections and artifacts, it hopes to foster an appreciation for baseball's cultural impact on society and honor the sport's many participants.

National Collegiate Athletic Association (NCAA)

700 W. Washington Street

P.O. Box 6222

Indianapolis, IN 46206-6222

(317) 917-6222

Web site: http://www.ncaa.org

Each of the NCAA's three divisions—Divisions I, II and III—creates its own rules governing personnel, amateurism, recruiting, eligibility, benefits, financial aid, and playing and practice seasons. Every program must affiliate its core program with one of the three divisions.

National Soccer Coaches Association of America (NSCAA)

800 Ann Avenue

Kansas City, KS 66101

(800) 458-0678

Web site: http://www.nscaa.com

FOR MORE INFORMATION

The NSCAA is the largest soccer coaches' organization in the world, with more than thirty thousand members who coach both genders at all levels of the sport. The NSCAA offers clinics and week-long courses nationwide, teaching more than six thousand soccer coaches each year.

Negro Leagues Baseball Museum
1616 East 18th Street
Kansas City, MO 64108
(816) 221-1920
(888) 221-NLBM (6526)
Web site: http://www.nlbm.com
The Negro Leagues Baseball Museum is a privately funded nonprofit organization dedicated to preserving the rich history of African American baseball. The museum is home to hundreds of photographs and artifacts and offers multimedia displays.

Olympic Hall of Fame and Museum
Canada Olympic Park
88 Olympic Park Road
Calgary, AB T3B 5R5
Canada
(403) 247-5452
Web site: http://www.winsportcanada.ca
This museum holds the largest collection of Olympic

memorabilia in all of Canada, including more than twenty Olympic torches dating back to the 1936 Berlin Games. Interactive displays such as the hockey shoot-out will test visitors' sport skills.

Pro Football Hall of Fame
2121 George Halas Drive NW
Canton, OH 44708
(330) 456-8207
http://www.profootballhof.com

The Pro Football Hall of Fame is dedicated to honoring those who have made outstanding contributions to professional football, preserving historic documents and artifacts, educating the public about professional football, and promoting the sport's positive values. Every year it inducts retired players, coaches, and owners.

WEB SITES

Due to the changing nature of Internet links, Rosen Publishing has developed an online list of Web sites related to the subject of this book. This site is updated regularly. Please use this link to access the list:

http://www.rosenlinks.com/gcsi/coach

FOR FURTHER READING

Austin, Krista, and Bob Seebohar. *Performance Nutrition: Applying the Science of Nutrient Timing.* Champaign, IL: Human Kinetics, 2011.

Berra, Yogi, with Dave H. Kaplan. *You Can Observe a Lot by Watching: What I've Learned About Teamwork from the Yankees and Life.* Hoboken, NJ: Wiley, 2008.

Biskup, Agnieszka. *Football: How It Works* (The Science of Sports). Mankato, ME: Capstone Press, 2010.

Burke, Dr. Louise, and Greg Cox. *The Complete Guide to Food for Sports Performance: Peak Nutrition for Your Sport.* Crows Nest, New South Wales, Australia: Allen & Unwin, 2010.

Dohrmann, George. *Play Their Hearts Out: A Coach, His Star Recruit, and the Youth Basketball Machine.* New York, NY: Ballantine Books, 2010.

Dungy, Tony, and Nathan Whitaker. *UnCommon: Finding Your Path to Significance.* Waterville, ME: Thorndike Press, 2011.

Ehrmann, Joe, Gregory Jordan, and Paula Ehrmann. *InSideOut Coaching: How Sports Can Transform Lives.* New York, NY: Simon & Schuster, 2011.

Garrido, Augie, and Kevin Costner. *Life Is Yours to Win: Lessons Forged from the Purpose, Passion, and Magic of Baseball.* New York, NY: Touchstone, 2011.

Green, Tim. *Football Genius.* New York, NY: HarperCollins, 2008.

Howard, Russ. *Curl to Win.* New York, NY: Harper, 2010.

Katz, Milton S. *Breaking Through: John B. McLendon, Basketball Legend and Civil Rights Pioneer.* Fayetteville, AR: University of Arkansas Press, 2010.

Krause, Jerry, with Don Meyer and Jerry Meyer. *Basketball Skills and Drills*. Champagne, IL: Human Kinetics, 2007.

Kush, Kevin, with Michael Sterba. *Competing with Character*. Boys Town, NE: Boys Town Press, 2008.

Lupica, Mike. *The Batboy*. New York, NY: Philomel, 2010.

Macy, Sue. *Swifter, Higher, Stronger: A Photographic History of the Summer Olympics*. Des Moines, IA: National Geographic Children's Books, 2008.

McCormack, Chris, and Tim Vandehey. *I'm Here to Win: A World Champion's Advice for Peak Performance*. New York, NY: Center Street, 2011.

Nicholson, Lorna Schults. *Winning Gold: Canada's Incredible 2002 Olympic Victory in Women's Hockey*. Victoria, BC, Canada: Lorimer Recordbooks, 2010.

Olsen, Leigh. *Going for the Gold: The 2008 U.S. Women's Gymnastics Team*. New York, NY: Price Stern Sloan, 2008.

Parrish, Kim D. *Cowboy Up: John Smith Leads the Legendary Oklahoma State Wrestlers to Their Greatest Season Ever*. Oklahoma City, OK: Oklahoma Heritage Association, 2007.

Richards, Ted. *Soccer and Philosophy: Beautiful Thoughts on the Beautiful Game*. Chicago, IL: Open Court, 2010.

Ross, Alan. *Second to None: The National Championship Teams of the Tennessee Lady Vols*. Nashville, TN: Cumberland House Publishing, 2007.

Roundtree, Sage. *The Athlete's Guide to Recovery: Rest, Relax, and Restore for Peak Performance*. Boulder, CO: Velo Press, 2011.

Ryan, Rex, and Don Yaeger. *Play Like You Mean It: Passion, Laughs, and Leadership in the World's Most Beautiful Game*. New York, NY: Doubleday, 2011.

Simon, Robert. *Fair Play: The Ethics of Sports*. Boulder, CO: Westview Press, 2010.

Smith, Leif, and Todd M. Kays. *Sports Psychology for Dummies*. Mississauga, ON, Canada: John Wiley & Sons Canada, 2010.

FOR FURTHER READING

Spizman, Justin, with Robyn Spizman and Nick Valvano. *Don't Give Up…Don't Ever Give Up with DVD: The Inspiration of Jimmy V—One Coach, 11 Minutes, and an Uncommon Look at the Game of Life*. Naperville, IL: Sourcebooks, 2010.

Sports Illustrated. *The Basketball Book by Editors of Sports Illustrated*. New York, NY: Sports Illustrated, 2007.

Thornton, Patrick K., Walter T. Champion, and Lawrence S. Ruddell. *Sports Ethics for Sports Management Professionals*. Burlington, MA: Jones & Bartlett Learning, 2011.

Walsh, Bill, and Steve Jamison. *The Score Takes Care of Itself: My Philosophy of Leadership*. New York, NY: Portfolio Trade, 2010.

Wooden, John, and Steve Jamison. *The Wisdom of Wooden: My Century On and Off the Court*. New York, NY: McGraw-Hill, 2010.

Wooden, John, with Don Yaeger. *A Game Plan for Life: The Power of Mentoring*. New York, NY: Bloomsbury, 2009.

BIBLIOGRAPHY

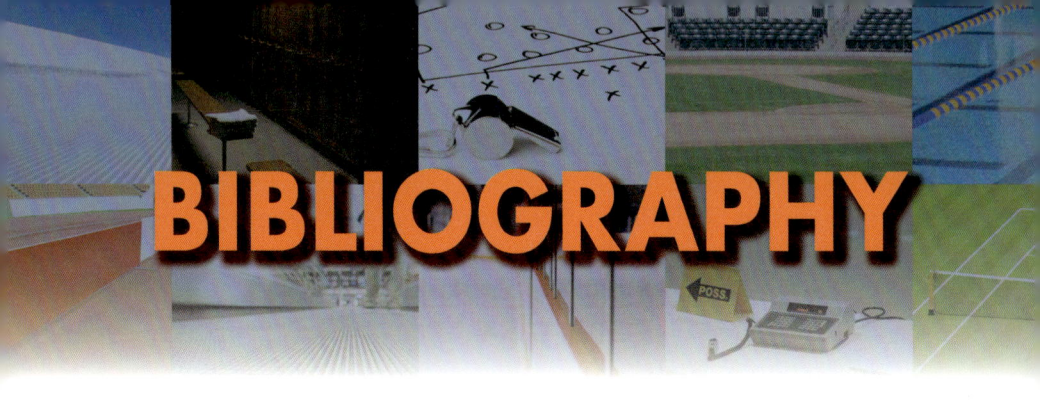

All American Speakers. "Biography of Bela Karolyi." Retrieved June 13, 2011 (http://www.allamericanspeakers.com/speakerbio/Bela_Karolyi.php).

American Sports Education Program with Joe Galat. *Coaching Youth Football.* Champagne, IL: Human Kinetics, 2010.

Bennet, Kyle. "All-time Winningest Coach Becomes a Spartan." MinaretOnline.com, March 24, 2011. Retrieved June 13, 2011 (http://theminaretonline.com/2011/03/24/article17291).

Black Coaches and Administrators. "Black Coaches and Administrators (BCA) Announces 2011 BCA Coach of the Year Awards." May 16, 2011. Retrieved June 13, 2011 (http://bcasports.cstv.com/genrel/051611aac.html).

Brown, Allen. "Rosselli to Help Coach USA at World Championships." WrestlingReport.com, September 8, 2011. Retrieved September 26, 2011 (http://wrestlingreport.com/current_news/viewtopic.php?f=17&t=29797).

BusinessPundit.com. "The 25 Highest Paid Sports Coaches in the World." November 16, 2009. Retrieved Sept 26, 2011 (http://www.businesspundit.com/the-25-highest-paid-sports-coaches-in-the-world).

Buzz Bissinger.com. "Friday Night Lights." Retrieved November 7, 2011. (http://www.buzzbissinger.com/friday-night-lights.html).

Clay, John. "In 29th Year, Kentucky Tennis Coach Still on Top of His Game." Kentucky.com, May 13, 2011. Retrieved June 13, 2011 (http://www.kentucky.

BIBLIOGRAPHY

com/2011/05/13/1739192/john-clay-in-29th-year-kentucky.html#ixzz1PDMgsj3X).

Clisso, Dion. "Coach Profile: SM West's Tim Callaghan 7/7." Prepskc.com, July 7, 2011. Retrieved September 24, 2011(http://www.prepskc.com/columns.php?id=751).

CoachK.com. "Quick Facts." Retrieved November 8, 2011. (http://coachk.com/meet-coach-k/quick-facts).

Dorfman, H. A. *Coaching the Mental Game: Leadership Philosophies and Strategies for Peak Performance in Sports, and Everyday Life*. Lanham, MD: Taylor, 2003.

Edwards, Daniel. "Palmeiras' Luiz Felipe Scolari Denies Interest in Sao Paulo Job." Goal.com, October 21, 2011. Retrieved November 8, 2011. (http://www.goal.com/en/news/584/brazil/2011/10/21/2722290/palmeiras-luiz-felipe-scolari-denies-interest-in-sao-paulo).

ESPN.com. "Summitt Stands Alone; Earns Milestone 1,000th Victory." February 5, 2009. Retrieved June 13, 2011(http://sports.espn.go.com/ncw/recap?gameId=290362633).

Evans, Thayer. "No Whistles, No Tackling, and No End in Sight." NYTimes.com, September 18, 2009. Retrieved June 13, 2011 (http://www.nytimes.com/2009/09/19/sports/ncaafootball/19coach.html).

Ferguson's Careers in Focus: Sports. New York, NY: Ferguson, 2004.

Field, Shelly. *Career Opportunities in the Sports Industry*. New York, NY: Checkmark Books, 2004.

Flaherty, James. *Coaching: Evoking Excellence in Others*. Wilburn, MA: Butterworth-Heinemann, 1990.

Garcia, Marlen. "Coach K Would Again Turn Down Shot at Coaching Lakers." USAToday.com, March 24, 2011. Retrieved November 8, 2011 (http://content.usatoday.com/communities/campusrivalry/post/2011/03/krzyzewski-lakers-coach-k-duke-nba/1).

TheGrio.com. "TheGrio's 100: Natalie Randolph, from Female Football Coach to Varsity Coach." February 1,

2011. Retrieved June 13, 2011 (http://www.thegrio.com/black-history/thegrios-100/2011-natalie-randolph.php).

HockeyCanada.com. "Melody Davidson to Be Inducted into Canadian Olympic Hall of Fame." February 9, 2011. Retrieved June 13, 2011 (http://www.hockeycanada.ca/index.php?ci_id=162339&la_id=1).

Maraniss, David. *When Pride Still Mattered: Lombardi*. New York, NY: Simon & Schuster, 2010.

Meyers, Dvora. "Last Leotard Standing." Slate.com, October 12, 2011. Retrieved November 8, 2011 (http://www.slate.com/articles/sports/sports_nut/2011/10/usa_gymnastics_injuries_the_united_states_women_keep_winning_gol.2.html).

National Baseball Hall of Fame and Museum. "Ryne Sandberg." Retrieved November 8, 2011. (http://baseballhall.org/hof/sandberg-ryne).

Navysports.com. "Navy Hires All-Time Winningest Volleyball Coach in NCAA History." January 18, 2011. Retrieved June 13, 2011 (http://www.navysports.com/sports/w-volley/spec-rel/011811aac.html).

OKState.com. "John Smith Profile." Retrieved November 8, 2011. (http://www.okstate.com/sports/m-wrestl/mtt/smith_john00.html).

Olney, Buster. "Don Meyer Set to Retire at End of Year." ESPN.com, February 22, 2009. Retrieved June 13, 2011 (http://sports.espn.go.com/ncb/news/story?id=4934150).

Perry, Tom. "College Football's 25 Highest Paid Coaches: Are They Worth It?" BleacherReport.com, May 27, 2010. Retrieved September 26, 2011 (http://bleacherreport.com/articles/393118-college-footballs-25-highest-paid-coaches-are-they-worth-it).

Potter, Joan. *African American Firsts: Famous Little-Known and Unsung Triumphs of Blacks in America*. New York, NY: Dafina Books, 2002.

BIBLIOGRAPHY

Rains, Rob. "Former Cardinals Coach Hal Lanier Finds Managerial Home in Independent League Baseball." Robrains.com, August 17, 2011. Retrieved September 26, 2011 (http://robrains.com/2011/08/former-cards-coach-hal-lanier-finds-managerial-home-in-independent-league-baseball).

Silby, Caroline, and Shelley Smith. *Games Girls Play: Understanding and Guiding Young Female Athletes*. New York, NY: St. Martins Press, 2000.

TideSports.com. "Nick Saban." Retrieved November 8, 2011. (http://alabama.rivals.com/viewcoach.asp?Year=2009&Sport=1&Coach=1924).

Van Riper, Tom. "The Highest-Paid College Basketball Coaches." Forbes.com, March 3, 2011. Retrieved September 25, 2011 (http://www.forbes.com/2011/03/03/highest-paid-college-basketball-coaches-business-sports.html).

Wooden, John. *Wooden on Leadership*. New York, NY: McGraw-Hill, 2005.

Wooden, John, with Steve Jamison. *My Personal Best: Life Lessons from an All-American Journey*. New York, NY: McGraw-Hill, 2004.

Wooden, John, with Don Yaeger. *A Game Plan for Life: The Power of Mentoring*. New York, NY: Bloomsbury, 2009.

YogiBerra.com "About Yogi." Retrieved June 13, 2011(http://www.yogiberra.com/about.html).

INDEX

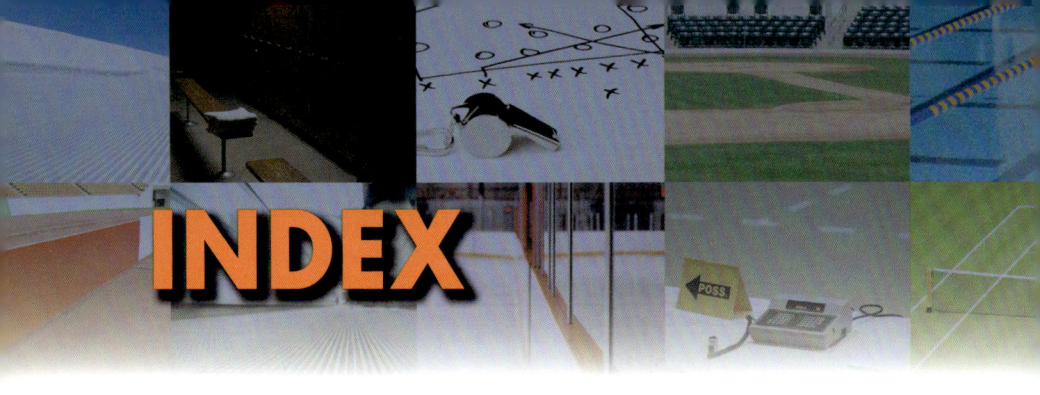

A

African American coaches, 32–33, 35–36
Alabama High School Athletic Association Hall of Fame, 91
Alberta Sports Hall of Fame, 47
Allison-Brewer, Nanabah, 20–21
American Basketball Association, 35
American Professional Football Association, 35
Arthur, Darrell, 6
Association of Middle Level Education (AMLE), 52
assistant coaches, 20, 23, 26, 33, 37, 47, 56–57, 62, 66, 67, 68, 70, 71, 75, 76, 77, 80, 81
athletic directors, 30, 59, 65, 67, 90

B

background checks, 54, 92
Basketball Hall of Fame, 35, 69
Bechard, Brennan, 37
Berra, Yogi, 79–80
Big 12 Conference, 5, 7
Black Coaches Association, 33
Blaik, Red, 23
Brown, Mack, 60
Brown v. Board of Education, 32

C

Calipari, John, 62
Callaghan, Tim, 44–45, 47–48
Canadian Association for the Advancement of Women and Sport Physical Activity, 47
Canadian Olympic Hall of Fame, 47
Chamberlain, Wilt, 33
Chaney, Don, 36
coaching
　career prep, 19–38
　certification, 49, 54, 57, 92
　college level, 60–71
　individual sports, 84–93
　middle/high school level, 50–59
　overview, 4–7

INDEX

professional level, 72–83
role in community, 8–18
salaries, 18, 55, 60, 62, 67, 70, 71, 76
Coaching Association of Canada, 47
College Football Hall of Fame, 14
Comaneci, Nadia, 87–88
community coaches, 39–49
Conroy, Pat, 69
CPR, 54, 92
Cunningham, Casey, 91

D

D'Antoni, Mike, 76
Davidson, Melody, 46–47
Davis, Al, 75
Davis, Ernie, 32–33
Ditka, Mike, 75
Dooley, John, 37
Dungy, Tony, 36

E

Embry, Wayne, 35
equipment managers, 28, 54, 66, 76

F

Ferguson, Sir Alex, 76
field managers, 72
Flores, Tom, 75

Forbes, Jeff, 37
Friday Night Lights, 56

G

Gagliardi, John, 13–14
Gagliardi Trophy, 13
Gaines, Clarence, 35
Ginn, Judith, 21

H

Heisman Trophy, 33
Hinson, Barry, 37
Hispanic coaches, 75

I

IKON/WBCA Coach of the Year, 69
Independent Women's Football League, 58
International Journal of Behavioral Nutrition and Physical Activity, 10
internships, 33–34, 38
Izzo, Tom, 62

J

Jack Donohue Coach of the Year Award, 47
Jackson, Darnell, 6
Jackson, Phil, 76
Jeffries, Willie, 35
Jimmy V. Perseverance Award, 63

John Bunn Award, 69
John Wooden Award, 5
Journal of Sports Management, 15

K

Karolyi, Bela, 87–88
Knight, Bobby, 69

L

Lanier, Hal, 77–78
Lombardi, Vince, 22–24
Lombardi Trophy, 23

M

Madden, John, 75
Major League Baseball (MLB), 35, 77
Manning, Danny, 5, 37
McKissick, John, 53
McLendon, John, 32, 35
McNamara, Julianne, 87
Meyer, Don, 63–64
Mills, Phoebe, 87
Minnesota Intercollegiate Athletic Conference (MIAC), 13
Mobile Sports Hall of Fame, 91
Moceanu, Dominique, 87, 88

N

Naismith College Coach of the Year, 69
National Association of Basketball Coaches, 5
National Association of Intercollegiate Athletics (NAIA), 35, 67, 71
National Baseball Hall of Fame, 80
National Basketball Association (NBA), 35, 36
National Collegiate Athletic Association (NCAA), 5, 7, 20, 25, 35, 38, 63, 64
National Football League (NFL), 23, 36, 75
National High School Athletic Coaches Association (NHSACA), 59
National High School Coaches Association, 91
Native American coaches, 20–21
Native American Sports Council, 21
no-cut programs, 52, 54, 86
North American Indigenous Games, 21
North American Society for Sports Management, 15

O

Okino, Betty, 87
Olympics, 8, 20, 32, 47, 69, 87–88
O'Neal, Buck, 35
operations, directors of, 37, 66
Owens, Jesse, 32

INDEX

P

Pan American Games, 68
Petro-Canada Coaching Excellence Award, 47
Pollard, Fritz, 35

R

Reilly, Rick, 36
Retton, Mary Lou, 87
Robinson, Frank, 35
Robinson, Jackie, 32
Robinson, Will, 35
Rosen, Natalie, 58
Rosselli, Lou, 91
Russell, Bill, 35

S

Saban, Nick, 60
scholarships, 13, 25, 33
Scolari, Luiz Felipe, 74, 76
Self, Bill, 5–6, 37
Smith, John, 91
Smith, Lovie, 36
sports instructors, 39–49
sports management, 15, 33–34, 36–37, 48, 71
Steinbrenner, George, 80
Stoops, Bob, 60
strength-training coaches, 66, 76
Strug, Kerri, 87, 88
Summitt, Pat, 68–69
Super Bowl, 23, 25, 36, 75

T

Tate, Jim, 90–91
Thompson, John, 35
Title IX, 58, 59

U

USA Gymnastics, 88
U.S. Sports Academy, 47
U.S. Youth Soccer, 42

V

Vivian Stringer Coaching Award, 47

W

WBCA/Converse Coach of the Year, 69
Western Athletic Conference (WAC), 20
White, Carol, 58
women coaches 20–21, 46–47, 58, 68–69
Wood, Jenifer, 42–43

Y

YMCA, 12, 41

Z

Zmeskal, Kim, 87, 88

ABOUT THE AUTHOR

Colleen Ryckert Cook is a writer and editor from Kansas City who has written several books for children and teens. She's calmed eager batters in the dugout, worked the down chains, and led dribbling drills for both soccer and basketball. On a good football day, when the air is crisp, the leaves orange, and the sky a shocking blue, she's been known to cry out to her team, "Make a wall of pain, boys!"

PHOTO CREDITS

Cover, p. 1 Hemera Technologies/AbleStock.com/Thinkstock; cover (background), pp. 1 (background), 49, 51, 70 Shutterstock.com; pp. 4–5 Tim Umphrey/Getty Images; p. 9 Paul Popper/Popperfoto/Getty Images; p. 11 Susan Leggett/Shutterstock.com; p. 16 Jupiterimages/Comstock/Thinkstock; p. 22 Chad McDermott/Shutterstock.com; p. 24 Tony Tomisc/Getty Images; pp. 27, 82, 87, 92 © AP Images; p. 31 Matt Henry Gunther/Taxi Japan/Getty Images; p. 32 Hulton Archive/Getty Images; p. 34 Joe Kohen/WireImage/Getty Images; p. 40 Comstock/Thinkstock; p. 46 Harry How/Getty Images; p. 55 Steve Liss/Time & Life Pictures/Getty Images; p. 57 © Clinton Wallace/Globe Photos/ZUMAPRESS.com; p. 61 Andy Lyons/Getty Images; p. 65 Greg McWilliams/Getty Images; p. 66 Quinn Rooney/Getty Images; p. 68 Jim McIsaac/Getty Images; p. 73 Peyton Williams/Getty Images; p. 74 Darren Walsh/Chelsea FC/Getty Images; p. 78 © Alan Look/Icon SMI; p. 79 Focus On Sport/Getty Images; p. 81 Pavel Shchegolev/Shutterstock.com; p. 85 Ronald Martinez/Getty Images; interior design elements: © www.istockphoto.com/hudiemm (grid pattern); http://lostandtaken.com (striped border); pp. 8, 19, 29, 39, 50, 60, 72, 84, 94, 96, 99, 105, 108, 113, 116, 120 (montage) © www.istockphoto.com, Shutterstock.com.

Designer: Brian Garvey; Editor: Bethany Bryan;
Photo Researcher: Karen Huang

Y 796.077 COOK

Cook, Colleen Ryckert.
Dream jobs in coaching

R4002054584 COL_PK

DISCARD

~~METROPOLITAN~~
Atlanta-Fulton Public Library